Iskwewak Kah' Ki Yaw Ni Wahkomakanak

Iskwewak Kah' Ki Yaw Ni Wahkomakanak

Neither Indian Princesses nor Easy Squaws

Second Edition

Dr. Janice Acoose-Miswonigeesikokwe

Women's Press
Toronto

Iskwewak Kah' Ki Yaw Ni Wahkomakanak: Neither Indian Princesses nor Easy Squaws, Second Edition
by Janice Acoose

First published in 2016 by
Women's Press, an imprint of Canadian Scholars' Press Inc.
425 Adelaide Street West, Suite 200
Toronto, Ontario
M5V 3C1

www.womenspress.ca

Library and Archives Canada Cataloguing in Publication

Acoose, Janice, author

    Iskwewak kah' ki yaw ni wahkomakanak : neither Indian princesses nor easy squaws / Dr. Janice Acoose-Miswonigeesikokwe. — Second edition.

Includes bibliographical references.

Issued in print and electronic formats.

ISBN 978-0-88961-576-2 (paperback).—ISBN 978-0-88961-577-9 (pdf).—ISBN 978-0-88961-578-6 (epub)

    1. Native peoples in literature. 2. Women in literature. 3. Canadian literature—History and criticism. 4. Native women—Canada. I. Title.
II. Title: Neither Indian princesses nor easy squaws.

PS8103.I6A26 2016   C810.9'352997   C2015-907957-8   C2015-907958-6

Text design by Integra
Cover design by Em Dash Design
Cover image: Leah Dorion, *Grandfather Sun Medicine* (2004), www.leahdorion.ca

Printed and bound in Canada.

Canadä

Table of Contents

Acknowledgements

This book is for my sons, Blair and Blue
And my grandchildren, Alijah, Angelina, Alizeah, and Lincoln
My sons, my grandchildren: you are the Eagle Bone whistles
Through which ancestral energies continue ...
My sons, my grandchildren: you inspire me each day to be
Miswonigeesikokwe

Revising this book has been necessary for me both personally and politically. Personally, it has been necessary because violence against women lives in our country, families, communities, and workplaces, feeding off racism, sexism, ignorance, fears, complacency, and secrets. Politically, it has been necessary because the numbers of missing and murdered Indigenous women in Canada continue to grow!

Whenever I write, I come to the page empowered with relations. So, I acknowledge here Kah' Ki Yaw Ni Wahkomakanak (all the Spiritual, other than human, and human relations) who continue to enrich my life. Specifically, I honour as Great-Spirited relations Nokomak Therese (Pelletier) Desjarlais, Philomene (Desjarlais) Beaudin, and Madeline (O'Soup) Acoose; my mother, Harriet (Beaudin) Acoose; my aunties, Edna (Beaudin) Henry, Marcella (Beaudin) Marquis, Agnes (Acoose) Agecoutay, Rosalie (Acoose) Lerat, Viola (Acoose) Delorme; my sisters, Iris, Vicky, Carol, Jackie, and Sandy; my nieces, Shawna, Amber, Sunshine, Maddie, Jessica Jayne, Jennie, Tawnee, Danna, Kristen, Shanna, Alicia, and Chelsea. Megweech for helping me to develop my Being as your great-granddaughter, granddaughter, daughter, niece, sister, and aunt. And, as I move forward into this challenging last chapter of my life, I've had support and encouragement from friends: thank you Christine Welsh, Moira Simpson, Rebecca Major, Diane Simpson, and April Chiefcalf. Also, thanks to my walking buddies Bruce Flamont, Jennifer Malmsten, and Sharon Feschuk. And, thank you Pat McCloskey for your beautiful photos.

8

Megweech to Canadian Scholars' Press/Women's Press for continuing to acknowledge and support my work. Thank you Natalie Garriga and Emma Johnson for your patience and encouragement.

Introduction

The ancestors were loud and getting louder ...
Sometimes [we] could hear them sing, other times they were crying out. Now
they seemed to just rattle.

—Winona Laduke, *Last Standing Woman*

Me and my sons, Blair and Blue, and grandchildren, Lincoln, Alijah-Blue,
Angelina, and Alizeah.

Before and after I speak or write, I show respect for all my Nehiowe-
Metis and Anishinaabe relations by acknowledging them as my
sources of cultural authority: for me, this is both a traditional and academic
practice. However, before placing ancestral names in this space, I clear the
textual ground to explain my use of terms. I use the word *Indigenous* as a
politically appropriate and literally correct term that confirms traditional
beliefs about Being originating from the land. To call attention to others' uses of "*Indian*," "*Native*," "*native*," "*First Nations*," "*Half-breed*," "*half-
breed*," "*Aboriginal*," and "*aboriginal*," I employ quotation marks to signal

their usage. I also use the words *white-eurocanadian-christian patriarchy*, which appear in lower case letters throughout this document to signal a politically motivated de-authorization of their prevailing ideology. When I use the words *signifying relations*, I mean a relational system that connects one's Being to specific cultures necessary for identity formation. Another word that requires some explanation is *relations*, which I use instead of *relatives* to maintain a colloquial, writerly voice. To me, the word *relations* feels more like the fluid, ever-changing relational system that helps me to understand my own Being. I also purposefully repeat the words *female signifying relations, re-membering*, and *dis-membering* throughout this document because I want to imitate, in my usage, ceremonial chants that when consistently vocalized encourage psychological and Spiritual change. Thus, in the context of memories, stories, and languages, the word *re-member/ing* signifies the re-creation and re-attachment of important relations for constituting Being to cultural bodies. Comparably, the word *dis-member/ing* refers to the strategic removal from cultural bodies signifying relations— in other words, Spiritual, other than human, and human relations who helped us understand our Being as culture-specific individuals. For example, in my usage of the old Anishinaabe word *Manitoukwe*, I mean Great-Spirited female relations whom I acknowledge as significant creators of life. And, when I use the Nehiowe words *Iskwewak Kah' Ki Yaw Ni Wahkomakanak*, I mean all my Spiritual, other than human, and human relations, to whom I ascribe the female gender and pronoun *she*.

My mother, Harriet (Beaudin) Acoose, was a Great-Spirited Nehiowe-Metis woman who raised five daughters and five sons during the social, economic, political, and Spiritual challenges of Canada's 1940s to the 1970s. The daughter of Philomene (Desjarlais) Beaudin and Fidele Beaudin, she was raised with strong cultural values, beliefs, and traditions. My mother's maternal grandmother was an equally Great-Spirited woman named Therese (Pittwawekanepitt) Pelletier, a Nehiowe from Cowessess First Nation. The daughter of Philomene Pittwawekanepitt and Dosithe Pelletier, my siblings and I remember Therese as "Down Koochum" (because she lived down the hill from my grandmother's house). Down Koochum is remembered by many Nehiowe-Metis and Anishinaabe in my Treaty #4 homeland as a Great-Spirited midwife with phenomenal knowledge and power of Spirits. Therese married Jimmy "Jacques" Desjarlais, the son of Bernard Desjarlais and Marie (Morin) Perreault from the Red River Metis homeland, St. Eustache parish. Mooshum Jimmy (as my siblings and I called him), together with Down Koochum, raised his family with a mix of Cree and Metis-christian values during Saskatchewan's early 1900s, in what subsequently became the Marival Half-Breed Colony. When their daughter Philomene took a husband, she married Fidele Beaudin, an orphan born to culturally French parents and subsequently raised by Oblate missionaries at Lebret, Saskatchewan. Once married to Marie, Fidele assimilated to her Nehiowe-Metis traditions and moved into Marival, a "half-breed" colony set up as a social laboratory with tightly controlled white-eurocanadian-christian-patriarchal dictates.

My paternal grandmother was Madeline O'Soup, a quietly determined Anishinaabekwe born to culturally Irish parents in the late 1800s. In infancy, she was orphaned and subsequently adopted by Chief Louis O'Soup and his wife from Saskatchewan's O'Soup Reserve (now the Cowessess First Nation). Madeline O'Soup married Paul Acoose in the early 1900s, and together they raised my father with a mix of Anishinaabe and christian values. Their relationship, and consequently my father, bore the effects of four generations of christian patriarchal supremacy. A form of white-eurocanadian-christian patriarchy was imposed on their lives through the Indian residential schools, ever-present priests and Indian agents, and Department of Indian Affairs agents. As a result of imposed christian-patriarchy, beyond my Koochum and Mooshum's generation, I have little knowledge of my female Anishinaabe relations. Fortunately, I do have knowledge of paternal male relations, such as Mooshum Samuel Acoose (great-grandfather) and Mooshum Quewich (great-great-grandfather), whom I came to know through oral stories passed on to me by Mooshum Paul Acoose (grandfather). Much later, as an undergraduate student, I would come to find the same stories of paternal relations in books written in English by Duncan Campbell Scott (early Canadian writer/Superintendent General of Indian Affairs/architect of the assimilation policy) and Edmund Morris (early Canadian frontier artist/son of the commissioner for the numbered treaties, Alexander Morris).

This book has been revised because of the growing numbers of missing and murdered Indigenous women in Canada, which I view as symptomatic of dis-membered relational systems resulting from christian patriarchal impositions. In this revised edition, I call attention to the ideology that fosters violence against Indigenous women because, as I write in the acknowledgements, it lives in our country, families, communities, and workplaces by feeding off of racism, sexism, ignorance, fear, complacency, and secrets. And, I connect the missing and murdered women to christian-patriarchy because I am a Nehiowe-Metis-Anishinaabekwe who has lived through an era in Canada that condoned blatant racism, sexism, and colonization. I thus make connections in this revised edition to the missing and murdered women in Canada, christian-patriarchy, literature, ideology, and cultural attitudes condoning violence to contribute to required immediate, necessary changes in policy development and legislation. I've added a new concluding chapter to show readers how to use the written text as a Creator-like Motherland for re-membering to Indigenous cultural bodies important signifying female relations for identity formation. I also include follow-up study questions to engage readers in necessary critical conversations that may contribute to the development of policies and legislation. Notably, in this revised edition, I acknowledge Iskwewak Kah' Ki Yaw Ni Wahkomakanak as Manitoukwe signifying relations for re-constituting Being.

My name, Miswonigeesikokwe, connects me to powerfully Spirited Nehiowe-Metis and Anishinaabe relations, whose accumulated strength and wisdom I continue to pass on to my sons and grandchildren. Re-membering my Being to such powerful female relations feels simultaneously painful and liberating, particularly when I write only in the colonizer's English language. The pain feels excruciating at times, because re-membering Being Nehiowe-Metis and Anishinaabe means reliving four generations of dis-membered relations under a rigid, racist, and sexist colonial regime. And, while I experience moderate waves of liberation as I deliberately and strategically re-member relations by writing in both my own languages and English, I struggle with Nehiowewin, Michef, and Anishinaabemowin conceptualization. My struggles are exacerbated by the white-eurocanadian-christian patriarchy's English language, which names my maternal culture Cree–"half-breed" rather than Nehiowe-Metis and my paternal culture Saulteaux rather than Anishinaabe. And, while I call on Manitoukwe relations when I attempt to write in my own languages, my Spirit battles with my mind because four generations of my family were subjected to specific colonial and christian strategies for dis-membering relational systems and languages. Four generations of my family were indoctrinated in white-eurocanadian-christian patriarchy, victimized by cultural repression/oppression in a "half-breed" colony and on a reserve, and imprisoned in christian residential schools. I try to overcome the battle between Spirit and mind by strategically decolonizing my writing, using non-sexist and non-racist language. And, I affirm my Being as a descendant of a long line of great Manitoukwe relations who gave me life.

At the time of this book's original writing, I was a mature university graduate student politically awakened by Indigenous writers throughout the Americas who wrote of white supremacy, imperialism, and colonization. One of these writers was Maria Campbell, whose fictionalized autobiography *Halfbreed* contextualized Indigenous people's social, political, and economic reality. Now, with a doctorate degree and specialty in Anishinaabe literature, I still think Campbell's *Halfbreed* is an important book. As a widely read Anishinaabe-Nehiowe-Metis scholar and critic, I understand the importance of Campbell's book for showing how writing in English can re-create and re-member signifying Indigenous female relations and revitalize cultural bodies.

Chapter 1 is a personal narrative that reveals white-eurocanadian-christian patriarchy as a powerful force of colonization operating on my life and relations. I recount the ways that Canada employed white-eurocanadian-christian patriarchy to strategically dis-member me from my Nehiowe-Metis-Anishinaabe cultural bodies and relations. I personalize this chapter to make clear the position from which I write and to reveal writing as a political act for reconstituting Being.

In chapter 2 I begin the process of reconstituting Being by deconstructing stereotypical images of Indigenous women. Accordingly, the chapter explores relationships between literature, stereotypes, and cultural attitudes. It also discusses some of the popular stereotypes of "Indian," "half-breed," and "Native" women that appeared in Canadian literature prior to

Me accepting my doctorate (acknowledgement of
Anishinaabe Literature specialist).

the publication of Maria Campbell's *Halfbreed* and other emergent voices
of Great-Spirited female creators.

Chapter 3 maintains that some eurocanadian literature imprisons
Indigenous women in stereotypes that perpetuate racism and sexism,
while imprisons fostering cultural attitudes that encourage violence against
Indigenous women. It also argues that those stereotypical images function
within the eurocanadian state as elements of an ideological apparatus that
violently severs Indigenous women from their cultural bodies. This chapter

attempts to eradicate such violence by creating a textual space for re-membering Indigenous women to culture-specific bodies, roles, and relations.

Chapter 4 focuses on two short stories by William Patrick Kinsella and Margaret Laurence: two highly effective and popular Canadian writers whose work continues to influence the global community. The chapter turns to Kinsella's "Linda Star" and Laurence's "The Loons" to show connections between literature, stereotypes, and cultural attitudes. It maintains that by relying on stereotypes, popular writers such as Kinsella and Laurence distort, fragment, and misrepresent realities of Indigenous women, consequently poisoning cultural attitudes towards Indigenous women in Canada. Rather than encouraging a ban on such works because they may encourage hate crimes against Indigenous women, this chapter uncovers, exposes, and lights up such places in both Kinsella's and Laurence's work to encourage readers to consider how literature shapes perceptions and colours attitudes.

Chapter 5 reveals Maria Campbell's fictional autobiography *Halfbreed* as intervening in the eurocanadian literary tradition and challenging existing stereotypes. It claims that even now, approximately 42 years after its first publication, it is an important book that illustrates how stories written in English can help us re-member Being. As such, the chapter shows Campbell using writing in English as a political act for decolonization, encouraging other Indigenous women to begin writing, to reclaim cultural memories and traditions, and thus reconnect to cultural bodies and relations.

Chapter 6 returns to the personal narrative format. As the book begins by adhering to cultural protocols, so too it concludes by acknowledging Kah' Ki Yaw Ni Wahkomakanak. It also returns to the personal narrative format to model possibilities for using English-language story forms as spaces for re-membering Being. Here it is important for readers to understand that I am not advocating English-language story forms as a replacement for culture-specific spaces and processes that constitute Being. I include the personal story in this final chapter to illustrate how my Nehiowe-Metis-Anishinaabekwe cultural Being continues to evolve in this multi-ethnic 21st-century Canadian nation, despite long-term strategies of cultural genocide employed by this country.

CHAPTER ONE

Iskwewak Kah' Ki Yaw Ni Wahkomakanak:
Re-membering Being to Signifying Female Relations

I dream for our people to stop dying, to stop feeling so alienated and so marginalized. I dream for our collective and individual well being.... We need liberation not only from the colonial legacy of the proverbial white man, we need liberation from our own untruths.
                —Emma LaRocque, *Contemporary Challenges*

Throughout my life I have been visited by powerful Spirits. During one visit, the Spirits of two old Koochums (grandmothers) came to me in a dream and beckoned me home. I responded to their Spiritual counsel by returning to my Nehiowe-Metis and Anishinaabe homelands. When at last my feet touched the earth from which I came, I felt the Spirits of Kah' Ki Yaw Ni Wahkomakanak (all my relations) welcome me home.

Following the directives from the Spiritual Koochums, I attempted, first, to re-member myself to maternal relations at my childhood Marival homeland, a "half-breed" colony set up in 1944 Saskatchewan during the "first socialist government in North America."[1] Whereas I remembered my childhood homeland as characterized by majestic rolling hills, luscious green trees, crystal-clear lakes, and bustling community life, now there was only tall dried grass, moved occasionally by wind and lonely animals. Undeterred by this stark reality, I searched a long time for my childhood home. Eventually, I found its decaying foundation buried in the earth, and as I tried to excavate memories, my fingers lovingly traced the concrete remains. Smells of the fecund earth re-membered me to important signifying maternal Nehiowe-Metis relations long gone to the realm of Spirits.

Hours later, on my second journey, I attempted to re-member myself to paternal relations on the nearby Sakimay "Indian" reserve. As soon as I arrived, relatives told me about the yearly Raindance, hosted by an old friend of my deceased father, Fred Acoose. Eager to participate, I respectfully adhered to Anishinaabe ceremonial protocol by seeking out the host and offering cloth and tobacco. He welcomed me immediately and encouraged me to take part in the celebration, subsequently instructing me to abstain from both food and water for the duration of the ceremony. Without the distraction of physical want, and with only my Spirit to guide me, over those few days I began to understand clearly the importance of re-membering Being to both maternal and paternal ancestors, and to empowering Spiritually other Indigenous families, communities, and nations. But I also came to the painful realization that, as a Nehiowe-Metis-Anishinaabekwe, I was heavily indoctrinated in white-eurocanadian-christian patriarchy. So, I asked the host to ceremonially re-member my Being to the Anishinaabe cultural body and relations by renaming me. To help prepare me Spiritually for the challenging journey ahead, he asked Elder Bill Standingready (from a neighbouring reserve) to rename me. As I arose re-membered to my cultural body as Miswonigeesikokwe, I felt strongly connected to the Great-Spirited Mother-Creator Aki (earth) and Kah' Ki Yaw Ni Wahkomakanak, but I wanted desperately for all my relations to become Spiritually and intellectually awakened. As University of Manitoba professor Dr. Emma LaRocque so eloquently writes, I "dream for our liberation in our land ... for our people to stop dying, to stop feeling so alienated and so marginalized. I dream for our collective and individual well-being."[2] Re-membered in ceremony as Miswonigeesikokwe, however, I felt empowered to begin my journey as Redsky Woman of the Bird Clan people from Sakimay First Nation.

FORM 1

DOMINION OF CANADA

REGISTRATION OF A LIVE BIRTH OF AN INDIAN

(Within the meaning of the "Indian Act" of Canada)

For use of Provincial Office only

901610 / 5 4

NOTE.—In case of more than one child at a birth, a Separate Registration must be made for each, and the number of each, in order of birth, stated.

Province... Saskatchewan

Agency in which birth took place...

1. PLACE OF BIRTH:

If on a Reserve... (Give name and location)

or If in a Rural Municipality... R.M. of ELCAPO No. 154 ... 000-05 (Give name or number)

or If in a City, Town or Village... Broadview ... Street... House No. (Give name)

and If in a hospital or institution... St. Michael's Hospital ... 26-16-5-W (Give name instead of street and number)

| 2. PRINT FULL NAME OF CHILD | Surname or last name: | A C O O S E |
| | All Given or Christian Names | M A R Y   J A N I C E |

| 3. Sex of child | 4. Single, twin, triplet, or other | 5. Are parents married to each other? | 6. Date of birth |
| Female | Single | Yes (Answer yes or no) | September (Month by name) 14 (Day) 19 54 (Year) |

7. PRINT FULL NAME OF FATHER ... ACOOSE (Surname or last name) ... FREDRICK (Given or Christian names)

8. Band or tribe to which father belongs... SAKIMAY

9. Residence of father... SAKIMAY RESERVE, GRENFELL, SASK. ... 000-05 (If on a reserve, give name and location)

10. Age last birthday... 31 ...years 11. Birthplace of father... SASKATCHEWAN (Province or country)

12. (a) Trade, profession or kind of work as teamster, trapper, canner, etc... Farmer

(b) Kind of industry or business as lumbering, fur trading, fish canning, etc... General

13. PRINT FULL MAIDEN NAME OF MOTHER ... BEAUDIN (Surname of last name) ... HARRIET (Given or Christian names)

14. Band or tribe to which mother belongs... SAKIMAY

15. Residence of mother... SAKIMAY RESERVE, GRENFELL ... 000-05 (If on a Reserve, give name and location)

16. Age last birthday... 27 ...years 17. Birthplace of mother... SASKATCHEWAN (Province or country)

18. (a) Trade, profession or kind of work as trapper, canner, etc... AT HOME

(b) Kind of industry or business as fur trading, fish canning, etc... (If unemployed, answer "At Home")

19. Children of this mother at the time of and including this birth:

(a) How many children of this mother are now living? 5

(b) How many children were born alive but are now dead? 0

(c) How many children were born dead? 0

20. Was this a premature birth? 0 If premature, length of pregnancy in weeks...

21. Name of doctor, nurse or other person in attendance at birth... A. H. CAMPBELL, M.D.

22. Marginal notations: (Office use only)...

23. I certify the foregoing to be true and correct to the best of my knowledge and belief.

Given under my hand at BROADVIEW this 20 day of SEPTEMBER 19 54

Signature of informant... Mrs. Harriet Acoose

Status of informant if other than parent...

Address... Grenfell Sask

24. I hereby certify that the above return was made to me at BROADVIEW, SASK.

on the... day of... 19...

Indian Agency No... Indian Agent

A copy of my birth certificate (notice "Live Birth of an Indian"!).

My ongoing journey towards liberation and empowerment has been a painful struggle that often leaves me feeling angry, resentful, frustrated, and confused. At numerous times throughout my journey, I have felt angry and resentful because of deliberate colonial, racist, and sexist strategies used to dis-member my Being from Nehiowe-Metis and Anishinaabe cultural bodies. I have also felt frustrated and confused throughout my life journey because white-eurocanadian-christian patriarchy is like a threatening spectre overshadowing community and family. Consequently, my own community and family were and are often rendered powerless against such strategic and institutionalized racism, sexism, and colonization, as my numerous contacts with white-eurocanadian-christian patriarchy illustrate below.

My first contact with white-eurocanadian-christian patriarchy was at birth in 1954 in Saskatchewan. After nine nourishing and loving months inside my Nehiowe-Metis mother's womb, I was delivered into a cold and sterile white-eurocanadian-patriarchal catholic hospital in Broadview. There, Grey (catholic) Nuns immediately imposed christian and patriarchal authority by stealing my mother's right to name me. And, just like my three older sisters, I was named Mary, becoming the fourth nominally indistinguishable female child in my immediate family to be named after the virginal mother of christ.

My second contact with white-eurocanadian-christian patriarchy was a few days after my birth on September 14, 1954. At that time, my birth was recorded on forms for the patriarchal bureaucracy as the "Registration of a Live Birth of an Indian," a legal process that registered me as an "Indian" and a genocidal process that dis-membered my Being from signifying Nehiowe-Metis-Anishinaabe cultural bodies and relations. And, while some people assume that status as a "registered treaty Indian" provides me with so-called lifelong privileges such as "free education" and "tax exemptions," I want to make two things very clear. First, the words *free education* and *tax exemption*, not unlike the words *easy squaw* and *Indian princess*, belong to a body of language used to justify racist beliefs about "Indians." Second, while I am a direct beneficiary of Treaty #4 signed at Fort Qu'Appelle, Saskatchewan, in 1876, the treaty (which some claim irrelevant to contemporary Canada) also directly benefits all Canadian residents who enjoy a level of wealth and legal protection created by their immigrant ancestors. Moreover, those same opportunities and protections are now extended to new immigrants, whose settlement in Canada has created an interesting multi-ethnic facade. It appears to be a politically constituted multi-ethnic nation, but at its centre, the country is still controlled and manipulated by white-eurocanadian-christian patriarchy. In regard to treaties, however, both old and new immigrants benefit. While some may quarrel with treaty rights being extended to the ever-growing Indigenous population, it's important to remember that treaties are binding and foundational legal documents, regardless of the changing social conditions. For clarity, I ask readers to consider Canadian mortgage agreements that borrowers enter into with lending institutions. When borrowers enter into mortgage agreements, they cannot arbitrarily change the terms and conditions. Moreover, homeowners cannot decide to stop paying their mortgage because they feel it irrelevant, unfair, or unjust. Unlike the lending and borrowing activity at the heart of this simple analogy, the process that imposed a treaty Indian legal status on me is rooted in a genocidal strategy for removing "Indians" from the land and dis-membering Being from signifying relations and cultural bodies. Thus, my second contact with white-eurocanadian-christian patriarchy dis-membered me from signifying maternal relations and usurped my right to legally identify as both Nehiowe-Metis and Anishinaabe.

The imposed legal identity as "Indian," like the historically imposed patronymic naming enforced in the late 1800s, was a colonial strategy to dis-member my Being from Nehiowe-Metis and Anishinaabe cultural bodies: the goal of such genocidal strategies was to disconnect "Indians" like myself from important signifying female relations. Prior to the imposition of colonial rule and white-eurocanadian-christian patriarchy, my Anishinaabe ancestors had their own personal names, which signified both clan and biological relations. In my paternal family, the name Acoose (or Ekos/Flying Bird) was my great-grandfather's personal and only name. Known for his running prowess, Ekos was so named because traditional Bonaise Doodaem (Bird Clan) Knowledge Keepers acknowledged his flying bird-like abilities as a runner. The son of Qu'wich, Ekos, was noted too as a powerful caller of Spirits, like his father. When he was christianized, Ekos was given the name Samuel Acoose, and all his descendants thereafter became Acoose. In other words, the change in naming to the pat-ronymic "Acoose" irrevocably disconnected our Beings from Anishinaabe Bonaise Doodaem relational systems that encouraged environmentally respectful ways of living and governance with all of Creation. Thus, under such a patriarchal system, I would subsequently be dis-membered from both important and signifying Anishinaabe Doodaem and Nehiowe-Metis female relations. There is still more evidence that shows how my peo-ple were disconnected from important signifying relations. In my pater-nal Sakimay First Nation home community, for example, there are very few people who re-member themselves to Bonaise Doodaem, much less acknowledge it as important for constituting Being. Also, in old colonial documents, in the spaces where our mothers' or fathers' names are to be inserted, the words "Indian," "half-breed," and sometimes "Indian squaw" appear. See, for example, my Down Koochum's application for "Half-Breed Scrip" below. Despite such genocidal attempts to dis-member me from signifying female relations, I was fortunate to have lived my life knowing my Down Koochum. Without that living connection to her, I could not re-member my Being (or any of my descendants) to the Nehiowe-Metis cultural body. As an Indigenous child, I was enriched Spiritually, intel-lectually, and physically with both Nehiowe-Metis and Anishinaabe rela-tions. The legal categorization as "Indian," imposed patronymic naming practices, and efforts to dis-member my Being from Great-Spirited female relations, however, traumatically altered my life.

My third contact with white-eurocanadian-christian patriarchy was a couple of months after my birth, when I was baptized in the catholic church. Baptized as a child of the male-god-he, I was brought into the catholic church as Mary Janice Georgiana Darlene Acoose, daughter of Mr. and Mrs. Fred Acoose, "Indians" from the Sakimay Reserve. Over the course of my life, I would understand the catholic church as one of the most powerful ideological colonial institutions operating on Indigenous peoples. In my communities, the catholic church wielded its ideological power through joyless, black-robed priests and nuns who closely scruti-nized all activities within the Marival Half-Breed Colony and the Sakimay Indian Reserve.

Form A.

Reserved *James Walker*

Disallowed
This Indian, married to a
Halfbreed, lives away from the
Reserve, but draws treaty.
The annuity to be commuted?

NORTH-WEST HALFBREED CLAIMS COMMISSION.
1900.

Before JAMES ANDREW JOSEPH McKENNA, of the City of Ottawa, in
the Province of Ontario, Esquire, and

JAMES WALKER, of the City of Calgary, in the North-West Territories, Esquire,

COMMISSIONERS,

duly appointed and sitting as a Royal Commission at *Fort Qu'Appelle*

in the North-West Territories, to investigate claims of Halfbreeds who were born in the
Territories between the 15th July, 1870, and the 31st December, 1885, personally came and

appeared *Philomine Pelletier*

Claimant, who being duly sworn, deposes as follows :—

Question 1. What is your name ?

Answer *Philomine Pelletier*

Question 2. Where do you reside ?

Answer *Crooked Lake N.W.T*

Question 3. Where were you born ?

Answer *On the North Saskatchewan River*

Question 4. When were you born ?

Answer *Twenty nine years ago*

Question 5. What is your father's name ?

Answer *O Pa_cha_pis* (*Indian*)

Question 6. What was the name of your mother before her marriage ?

Answer *Sauteaust* (*Indian*)

Question 7. Is your father a Halfbreed or an Indian ?

Answer *Indian*

Question 8. Is your mother a Halfbreed or an Indian ?

Answer *Indian*

Question 9. Have you ever received land or scrip in Manitoba or the North-West
Territories in commutation of your Halfbreed rights ?

Answer *No*

A copy of my Down Koochum's "Half-Breed Scrip" application.

My fourth contact with white-eurocanadian-christian patriarchy was in 1959 in Saskatchewan. I was five years old when I was imprisoned behind the drab and dreary walls at the Cowessess "Indian" Residential School. The effects of my four-year imprisonment (1959–1963) and the Spiritual, psychological, physical, and sexual abuse that accompanied it, as well as the strategic programmed terrorism disguised as education and christianization, *live* in me, as a diagnosed psychological condition: post-traumatic stress disorder (PTSD). In my family, like in many other "Indian" families, legally sanctioned imprisonment and programmed terrorism began in the late 1800s with my great-grandparents, and our legacy as "Indians" was carried on into my grandparents' lives, passed on to my father and his siblings, and then to me and my siblings. Anishinaabe scholar Lawrence Gross astutely describes such collective trauma as post-apocalyptic stress disorder (PASD), when PTSD lives in entire cultures over many generations.[3]

The day my mother delivered my siblings and me to the Cowessess "Indian" Residential School still haunts my memories. I'm haunted by memories of black-robed priests and nuns who terrorized me into submission. I have haunting memories of my mother being pushed out the door with a stern warning from the nuns not to get emotional about saying goodbye. I'm haunted, too, by echoes of my own screams, crying out for my mother and clinging tightly to my sister as the nun read through all the rules, which I seldom remembered and was consequently punished for disobeying. One of the rules, we quickly learned, was that boys and girls were to be completely segregated. Thus, my four-year imprisonment in the Cowessess "Indian" Residential School haunts me still, because I have painful memories of seeing my brother Fred, caged like an animal behind a barbed-wire fence I passed on my way to class. I'm haunted by memories of that first day of school, too, because I can still feel being ripped away from my sisters, herded down a long, dark hall, pushed into a room to have my hair shorn, powdered with DDT insecticide (supposedly because all "Indians" were infected with lice), and then showered with severely hot water.

Once stripped of remembrances of home, I was given a number, a school uniform, and an assigned bed in the "small girls' dormitory." Over

This was the day my sister Mary Carol and I went to the "Indian" Residential School. Brother Clem is in between us. Photo credit: Harriet Acoose

the years, programmed terrorism effectively encouraged me to respond to the number rather than my name. The school uniform, too, stripped me of any individual identity. The army-like bunk to which I was assigned at least provided me with some small comfort, since it was positioned close to my older sister, Mary-Madeline. As part of the nighttime rituals, the nuns ordered me to always sleep facing right, with hands folded in a praying position under my head. Although it was monotonous and sometimes torturous, the daily routine helped me to survive from one day to the next. Each day I awoke very early, recited prayers, showered, dressed, ate meals (prefaced by prayers), attended catechism and school (prefaced by more prayers), and took part in rigidly programmed physical exercises. Bedtime was welcome after excruciatingly painful periods of time endured on our knees in prayer circles. And, although I cried myself to sleep at night, crying became part of the rituals that helped me to survive. Some nights I cried myself to sleep because I longed to be at home with my family. Other times I cried at night because I remembered daily physical punishments: sometimes my mouth and face were slapped; sometimes my knuckles were pounded with a wooden block; and sometimes my mouth was taped shut for long periods of time. Too many times I was physically punished and psychologically terrorized for speaking out of turn, asking too many questions, or showing "disrespect" for their god by asking for proof of "his" existence. The nuns' consistent nighttime threats of eternal damnation, as well as haunting visits from satan himself and desperate Spirits from purgatory, intensified my fears. Other times I cried in terror when I heard footsteps creeping up the fire escape to our little girls' dormitory. Those nights I jumped into my sister Mary-Madeline's bed and clung to her fiercely for protection as I listened to little girls' tortured whimpers, muffled screams, and desperate cries for help. I remember trying to tell anyone who would listen about those night visits to our dorm, the cruel punishments, and the deadly threats, but my voice was silenced by family fears, community pressure, and church power. Even now, as a chronic insomniac, a part of me still struggles to overcome such psychological terrorism. As the beneficiary of four generations of programmed terrorism inflicted through the residential school, I began to doubt what I believed, felt, and saw. Those feelings were reinforced throughout my life by comments such as "Surely the residential schools accomplished some good; didn't you learn to read and write?" which I now reason only masked the speaker's years of pent-up discomfort and collective guilt.

Programmed terrorism through the "Indian" residential school began when I was a five-year-old child in the formative developmental years of my life. It continued on through the years until I was nine, by then effectively programmed through terrorism to reject my cultures, languages, history, and ancestors. How was I to comprehend at five years of age that forcing me to speak English rather than my own languages was part of a terrorist program that would alter my psyche and identity? How was I to comprehend the effects of programmed terrorism upon three previous

The Cowessess "Indian" Residential School I attended from 1959 to 1963.

familial generations forced to reject Spirituality, history, stories, and languages? Or how those seemingly innocent stories about Dick, Jane, Spot, and Puff from our Grade 1 and 2 readers served an ideological system much different from my own? I'm sure it confused me when I could not see reflections of my own wonderfully alive home life, especially since I did not have a language to name and link such literary tools to a terrorist program for "killing the Indian." How was I to understand that representations of quietly reserved, pleasantly passive, and submissive ladies in those early books were part of a body of stereotypes employed to foster white-supremacist cultural attitudes? How was I to understand, too, those seemingly simple "spot the difference" exercises from phonics workbooks as part of an "othering" process that placed me outside the ideal fostered in textbooks? I certainly did not understand the location of my "self" as marginalized, nor how such marginalization would make me feel ashamed and dis-membered from signifying relations. I'm sure it confused me even more to not find representations in school books of those Great-Spirited female relations who signified cultural Being. My homes (both the "Indian" reserve and the "half-breed" colony) were constantly enriched with female relations who thought nothing of making room for another hungry person at our already overcrowded supper table, or casually throwing blankets on the floor for visitors to sleep. Thinking back over the years, I realize now that representations of Great-Spirited Indigenous female relations rarely appeared in the pages of history books, even though they actively participated in the early development of this country. Without such cultural referents in books written in English, my fourth contact with white-eurocanadian-christian patriarchy in 1959 in Saskatchewan significantly altered my cultural Being.

Throughout my life, my cultures (which were too often misrepresented as racially "Indian"), gender, Spiritual practices, and economic status set me apart from mainstream society, whose ideological power fostered exclusiveness. I felt set apart from mainstream society during my high school years between 1969 and 1973 at Miller Comprehensive High School in Regina, Saskatchewan. While most Canadians look back on their high school experience as a time for maturing development, my time at Miller Comprehensive High School was poisoned by institutional racism and sexism, ever-present in mainstream student and teacher attitudes, pedagogical strategies, and textual ideology. At that time, I did not have the political consciousness or strength of Spirit to challenge contemporaneous pedagogy or the school's dominating racism and sexism, and I therefore internalized inferiority and shame. And, not unlike so many other Indigenous women who suffer psychological, economic, Spiritual, political, and physical traumas associated with colonialism, sexism, and racism, I shamefully turned away from my history and cultures, believing that I was an easy squaw and "Indian" whore who deserved to be repeatedly violated and raped by white priests, teachers, psychologists, and other men.

Many frustrating and challenging years later, I was Spiritually reborn and politically awakened. I was reborn and awakened in part by politically astute, culturally tenacious, and Spiritually strong Indigenous activists throughout the Americas, whose collective voices empowered me to challenge the prevailing white-eurocanadian-christian patriarchy's institution of higher learning. I remember vividly that first day in 1986 when I walked through the front doors of the University of Saskatchewan's Place Riel as a politically awakened and Spiritually reborn Indigenous woman. Still aware of the effects of programmed terrorism, I felt haunted by white-christian-canadian patriarchy and shadowed by ignorant, uncivilized, savage, barbaric, heathen, dirty, pagan, drunk, no-good "Indian," and easy squaw stereotypes as I made my way to classes. And, even though I felt politically empowered, once inside the classroom I realized that pedagogical strategies, required textbooks, and some of the professors still served a white-eurocanadian-christian patriarchy. Indeed, there were plenty of professors at the University of Saskatchewan in various disciplines who implicitly and explicitly reinforced notions of white cultural supremacy, albeit perhaps unconsciously, ignorantly, or naively.

When I contemplate the way that professors implicitly and explicitly reinforced notions of white cultural supremacy, I'm reminded of two incidents that happened at the University of Saskatchewan with two sessional instructors. The first incident occurred on day one of a fur trade history class. As the instructor reviewed his selected readings, he spoke of "Indian" women and fur traders. And, without even a bit of consideration, he characterized the "Indian" women as sexually promiscuous. When I asked him to reconsider his comment, given the obvious interpretive white-christian-male bias, he made great attempts to silence me. First, he said very matter-of-factly, "No, I don't have to consider what you call bias." Second, he did not encourage further discussion. Third, he moved very quickly onto another topic. So, rather than sit through a whole term enduring racism and sexism, I dropped the class. The second incident involved a sessional instructor hired to teach a western Canadian literature class. Upon signing up for the class, I was absolutely astounded to find that he had excluded a significant body of work by Indigenous authors. So, I made an appointment to speak to him. For what I perceived to be a confrontation, I prepared myself emotionally, Spiritually, and physically, like a fierce Okichita (Anishinaabe woman warrior). Ready for battle, I asked him why he had not included Indigenous writers on his list of required reading. In contrast to my warrior-woman posturing, he answered me in a typically confident white-male academic voice, "There are none that are quite good enough." Not easily dissuaded, I confronted him, too, about the words "from no man's land to every man's land," a phrase used in the "course description" section of his syllabus. I tried to explain that I felt very angry and frustrated at the description of the prairies as "no man's land," and I told him that I was frustrated and angry at his and the institution's casual dismissal of my Nehiowe-Metis and Anishinaabe ancestors (both female and male) who had cared for and nurtured the land since time immemorial. Although I left his office feeling the matter was unresolved, I made a personal commitment to complete his class. Later, I would write a term paper about the unrealistic, derogatory, and stereotypic images of Indigenous people that appeared in books selected for his western Canadian literature reading list. In fact, the ideas for my master's thesis were born from that battle with him. Years later, the same instructor told me that he had learned some things from my time in his class. And, when he recounts that time to others, he tells them that he has "been suitably Acoosed," which I'm not sure is a compliment or an insult.

My decision to study at the graduate level in the University of Saskatchewan's Department of English was part of a political strategy to challenge Canada's prevailing white-christian-canadian patriarchal ideological assumptions, too often encountered through classroom experience and the books included as "required readings." I became very zealous about challenging unrealistic, derogatory, and stereotypic images of Indigenous peoples in literature, and I was empowered by scholars such as Dr. Emma LaRocque to speak out and "self-express because there was so much about our history and about our lives that ... has been disregarded, infantilized, and falsified."[4] Like LaRocque, "I think I had this missionary zeal to tell about our humanity because Indian-ness was so dehumanized and Metis-ness didn't even exist."[5] And whereas most graduate students feel they have very little power, I felt empowered by Indigenous writers, activists, and Kah' Ki Yaw Ni Wahkomakanak. The Spiritual energies of all my relations, the political actions of activists, and the voices of scholars and activists fuelled my educational journey, and so I began to develop ideas for Indigenizing the University of Saskatchewan generally, and the Department of English specifically. The only Indigenous woman in a program that, at least to my perception, appeared unwelcoming and resistant to pedagogic change, I sometimes felt like an avian ancestor removed from the sky world, unprotected, alone, and isolated. On numerous occasions when I challenged a selected text's unrealistic, derogatory, and

Me when I received my master's degree.

stereotypic images, I certainly felt the authoritative strength and power of white-eurocanadian-christian patriarchy.

Eventually, I realized that doing the kind of work I had set out to do for my master's thesis required a lot of support. My strongest support and encouragement came from Dr. Ron Marken and Dr. Susan Gingell, two compassionate and committed activist-educators. Their support, along with the Spiritual energies of Kah' Ki Yaw Ni Wahkomakanak and many traditional Knowledge Keepers, family, friends, and professional associates, fuelled my energies to challenge the ideological basis of the Canadian education system generally, and its literary canon specifically. During the first few minutes of my master's thesis defence, I spoke about my insecurities and explained that I felt somewhat powerless as an Indigenous woman struggling against hundreds of years of white-eurocanadian-christian patriarchy. Such feelings were intensified when one of the members of my graduate committee described my work/ideas/words as "very abrasive and disturbing" to him as a white-christian male. And, while at first his comments unsettled me, eventually I felt a renewed commitment to intelligently sensitize those gathered at my defence. I spoke at length about the Spiritual, emotional, and physical pain and frustration I had endured over the years studying in the English department. Some time later, however, I felt victorious as the first Nehiowe-Metis-Anishinaabekwe to graduate with a master's degree (and now a PhD) from that department. I also felt victorious because my studies and developing critical skills helped me to begin the process of re-membering Being to Manitoukwe and Kah' Ki Yaw Ni Wahkomakanak.

Essentially, in my thesis, "Iskwewak: Kah' Ki Yaw Ni Wahkomakanak," out of which the first edition of this book grew, I argue that Canadian literature is an ideological instrument. As an ideological instrument, Canadian literature promotes the cultures, philosophies, values, religion, politics, economics, and social organization of white, european, christian, canadian patriarchy while fostering cultural attitudes about Indigenous peoples based on unrealistic, derogatory, and stereotypic images. My own experience in mainstream university literature classes taught me a number of critical lessons that I carry with me into the classrooms where I now teach. It taught me, first of all, that literature and books are powerful political tools. Because literature and books are powerful and political, I encourage students to read critically and with an awareness of their own cultural position. I realized, however, that most university students are not critical readers, thinkers, and writers on the subject of "Indians," "Eskimos," or "half-breeds." Consequently, many come to "know" Indigenous peoples only through highly selective images perpetuated through a similarly highly selective literature, which ultimately maintains the white-euro-christian-canadian status quo.

Experience in mainstream university literature classes also taught me valuable lessons about the relationship between language and power. Through my studies, I came to the conclusion that the English language is first and foremost the language of colonizers, although some contemporary scholars argue that it is also now an Indigenous language. In "Theorizing American Indian Experience," Craig Womack writes, "I do not think it a certainty that the English language is the colonizer's language. Once it landed in the New World, English picked up a lot of tribal influences from Indians, from Africans in the Caribbean, and so on. Literally there are thousands of Indian words in English. Maybe Indians colonized English instead of the other way around."[6] I agree with Womack that the English language has, like all languages, evolved to reflect social, economic, and political changes. What hasn't changed is that English continues to serve the interests of those in power: consider, for example, the influence of English internationally. In my interactions over the years with legal, educational, or communication institutions, I observed that white-eurocanadian-patriarchal interests are protected and served through English. Consider how English still upholds white-eurocanadian-christian power, as in its most important signifying male god, "he." In recent years, I have become enthused by feminist scholars' significant challenges to patriarchal language and power, particularly those Indigenous women scholars who dare to attach the word *feminist* to their scholarly work and identity.

As I am a politically awakened and widely read Nehiowe-Metis-Anishinaabekwe feminist, I can no longer ignore the effects of colonization, racism, and sexism. As I stated previously, my awakening began when I was newly re-membered to my own cultural bodies. I was also awakened politically by Indigenous activists throughout the Americas who inspired me to speak, act, and write. Thus, when I began my career as an educator, my first political act was to subvert white-eurocanadian-christian patriarchy in the selections for my required reading list for predominantly Indigenous first-year English students. Because I wanted students to make connections to the texts, to interact with them, I felt they needed to see realistic representations of themselves. So, instead of requiring them to read so-called canonical authorities such as Chaucer, Milton, Jonson, Donne, Pope, Shakespeare, Wordsworth, Swift, Dickens, Whitman, Melville, Faulkner, or Hemingway, to provide them with an historical and cross-cultural reading experience I now rely on Indigenous Knowledge Keepers. Thus, I encourage my students to read Kahgegagahbowh (Anishinaabe), Pauline Johnson (Mohawk), Joe Dion (Cree), Maria Campbell (Metis), Louise Halfe (Cree), Marie Annharte Baker (Anishinaabe), Beth Cuthand (Cree), Jeannette Armstrong (Okanagan), Tomson Highway (Cree), Lenore Keeshig-Tobias (Anishinaabe), Drew Hayden Taylor (Anishinaabe), Winona LaDuke (Anishinaabe), Louise Erdrich (Anishinaabe), Marilyn Dumont (Metis), Richard Wagamese (Anishinaabe), Paul Seesequasis (Metis-Cree), Robert Warrior (Osage), Craig Womack (Oklahoma Creek–Cherokee), Jace Weaver (Cherokee), and Gregory Scofield (Metis). Finding reflections of their own lives in the selected readings empowers students when they see how Indigenous knowledge is evolving, intelligent, and contributing to the world community. Using Indigenous-authored texts, I also show students how contemporary Indigenous writers use contemporary literary forms to re-member and recreate Indigenous cultures and relations while simultaneously remaining connected to essential Spiritual values and traditions.

Sisters Sandy and Jackie on Mom's knee, and from left to right in the back, sister Carol, niece Shawna, me, and sister Vicky.

CHAPTER TWO

Literature, Stereotypes, and Cultural Attitudes

You are not good enough, not good enough, obviously not good enough.
The chorus is never loud or conspicuous,
just there.
　　　　　—Marilyn Dumont, "Memoirs of a Really Good Brown Girl"

Great-Spirited literary female-creators such as Marilyn Dumont (Metis), Mourning Dove (Colville-Okanagan), Gertrude Bonnin (Yankton-Sioux), Paula Gunn Allen (Laguna Pueblo–Sioux), Mary Brave Bird (Lakota-Sioux), Elizabeth Cook-Lynn (Dakota-Sioux), Ella Deloria (Yankton-Sioux), Maria Campbell (Metis), Emma LaRocque (Metis-Cree), Louise Halfe (Cree), Beth Cuthand (Cree), Beth Brant (Mohawk), Pauline Johnson (Mohawk), Marie Annharte Baker (Anishinaabe), Winona LaDuke (Anishinaabe), Louise Erdrich (Anishinaabe), Lenore Keeshig-Tobias (Anishinaabe), Linda Hogan (Chickasaw), Joy Harjo (Muskogee Creek), Leslie Marmon Silko (Laguna Pueblo), Lee Maracle (Metis), and others have forever altered the way that Indigenous relations are created in books written in English throughout the Americas. Before the genesis of such bodies of literature, Indigenous women were represented in Canadian and American literature between the polemical stereotypical images of the "Indian" princess—an extension of the noble savage—and the easy squaw—a contemporary distortion of the squaw drudge.

These literary representations create very powerful images that perpetuate stereotypes and, more importantly—as is apparent in the growing
numbers of missing and murdered women in Canada—foster dangerous
cultural attitudes that condone violence against Indigenous women. This
chapter therefore challenges readers, first, to put aside their assumptions
about literature, and particularly the frequently encountered idea of its
apolitical aesthetic character. Second, this chapter encourages readers
to think critically about the relationship between text and stereotypes,
with a view to understanding how their own cultural attitudes towards
Indigenous women have been shaped by literature, an apparatus of the
prevailing white-eurocanadian-christian-patriarchal ideology. Third, this
chapter delineates relationships between literature, stereotypes, and
cultural attitudes by exploring the history of Indian princess and easy
squaw stereotypes, and positing their existence by looking to some of the
European traditions in which they were constructed.

A review of early Canadian literature reveals clear connections between
christian patriarchy, liberalism, and stereotypic images. My reading of the
early Canadian literary canon reveals politically motivated support for the
developing nation's christian-patriarchal ideology. As the canon evolved, it
reflected a growing secular liberalism, which modified, and to some extent
replaced, fundamental christian dogmatism. Used here, the term *liberalism* means a political movement born out of ongoing struggles with church
authority, transplanted into the developing Canadian nation, and manifested in state policies and practices. The term is also used as Kenyan writer
Ngugi Wa Thiong'o defines it: "the sugary ideology of imperialism," because
it dominates Canadian academia and continues to strongly influence writers' textual constructions.[1] As it appears in early Canadian literature, liberalism reveals itself, to borrow Thiong'o's phrasing, blurring "all antagonistic
class contradictions, all the contradictions between imperialistic domination
and the struggle for national liberation, seeing in the revolutionary violence
of the former, the degradation of humanity."[2] In other words, liberalism
appears in the literature as covertly justifying imperialist practices.

My analysis of european-christian-patriarchal liberal traditions (out of
which early Canadian literature grew) illuminated for me the origins of
Indian princess and easy squaw stereotypes. In my search for the roots of the

Indian princess and easy squaw stereotypes, I realized that the word *ideology* (used in this document to mean a very basic way of understanding, reflecting a particular group's way of being, knowing, seeing, and being in the world) is of primary importance. Thus, I found Robert Berkhofer's *The White Man's Indian* to be a useful source for understanding ideological constructs of "Indians," including the squaw and princess stereotypes. He claims that "European" explorers such as Christopher Columbus were fuelled by adventurous dreams of expansionism and potential mercantile profits before they arrived in the New World, and their ideological views of New World peoples were constructed from within a 15th-century european-christian patriarchy, which Berkhofer specifically describes as "familiar conceptual categories and values."[3] Berkhofer concludes, therefore, that images of the "Indian," like the term itself, came from Columbus's erroneous cartography.

The most detailed New World ethnography, according to Berkhofer, came from Amerigo Vespucci's *Mundus Novus*, published about 1504 or 1505. Vespucci's work is important for the study of the Indian princess and easy squaw stereotypes because his writings mark the beginnings of a white-christian-male bias. Indigenous women's imprisonment in sexist and racist stereotypes may be traced partly to Vespucci, who wrote that when Indigenous women "had the opportunity of copulating with Christians, urged by excessive lust, they defiled and prostituted themselves."[4] His work also contains interesting contradictions between christian morality and personal desire when he describes naked women's bodies as "barely tolerably beautiful and clean." His words seem to suggest both a desire for and revulsion of Indigenous women, although such feelings and inclinations are undermined by his revulsion of Indigenous women, whom he believed to be prostituting themselves.[5] His observations, in my opinion, influenced the creation of early white-euro-christian patriarchy's promiscuous, princess, and squaw stereotypes and cultural bias. Transplanted into Canada and its institutions, like literature, such stereotypes came to be the standard upon which representations of Indigenous women were based.

A couple of other useful sources for understanding connections between literature, stereotypes, and cultural attitudes are Raymond

William Stedman's *Shadows of the Indian: Stereotypes in American Culture*[6] and Angelika Maeser-Lemieux's "The Metis in the Fiction of Margaret Laurence: From Outcast to Consort,"[7] both of which connect stereotypic representations to imperialism and colonization. Like Berkhofer's work, Stedman's and Maeser-Lemieux's work leads me to believe that stereotypes of "Indian" women fostered cultural attitudes that promoted European interests during the historical era of imperialism and colonization. Before a so-called good christian whiteman could have relations with an "Indian" woman, however, she had to become a "good" Indian princess. For example, Dona Marina (Aztec), who had a liaison with Hernando Cortez, is represented as the daughter of a "native" nobleman. Pocahontas (Powathan), who liaised with John Smith, is represented as "Princess" Pocahontas. Like Berkhofer, who includes 16th-century artist Stradanus's illustration of a scantily clad young maiden "rising from her hammock to greet Americus Vespucci," Stedman's work provides plausible connections to the princess stereotype and its employment for the colonial agenda.[8] To reinforce such plausible connections, Stedman includes in his text various images of barely clothed Indigenous women that appeared in illustrations symbolizing the New World, imperialism, and colonization. He includes, for example, an Amazonian-type woman with spear and severed head, dated 1581; a regal-looking woman with bow and arrow sitting on top of an armadillo, dated 1594; and a majestic-type woman in a carriage pulled by two armadillos, dated 1644. Another compelling source that traces connections between literature, stereotypes, and cultural attitudes is Maeser-Lemieux's essay, which draws on Rayna Green's (Cherokee) "The Pocahontas Perplex: The Image of Indian Women in American Culture." Maeser-Lemieux points out that stereotypically "the Indian Queen was presented as a symbol of the Americas which, after the colonial period in the United States, became divided into the figures of Princess or Squaw."[9] As I read Stedman and Maeser-Lemieux, both the good Indian woman (or the Indian princess archetype) and the bad "Indian" woman (or the shadowy, lustful squaw archetype) stereotypes foster cultural attitudes that justify imperialistic expansion and the colonial agendas of explorers, fur traders, and christian missionaries.

My selected reading of some of the Hudson's Bay Company (HBC) fur trade records and Jesuit missionary correspondences also led me to reason that such documents fed 19th-century obsessions with the good princess and bad squaw stereotypes. For example, the HBC documents and the Jesuit Relations and Allied Documents (JRAD), used often by historians, encouraged the constructed stereotypic images of Indigenous (Canadian) peoples. And, while HBC records are primarily business transactions between the company and "Indian" fur traders, and JRAD letters are primarily from Jesuits requesting resources from their colonial home office, these documents are too often used as sources of historical facts. That is to say that historians and writers too often ignored obvious white-male-christian-patriarchal bias, interpreting information contained in the documents as historically accurate. Peter C. Newman's discussion of relations between "Indian" men, company men, and "Indian" women in *Company of Adventurers* exemplifies a typical historian's reliance on such biased documents. In one passage, he writes about George Nelson, an observant Nor'Wester who described "the bitter lament of an Indian who hoped to pass off his second wife to a white man because he considered her to have been debauched by past associations with them."[10] According to Newman's selective use of fur trade records, Indigenous women appear in his book as "sluts—to satisfy the animal lust, and when they [the men] are satiated, they cast them off, and another one takes her ... until she becomes an old woman, soiled by everyone who chuses to use her."[11] While some scholars (at the time of this book's original writing), such as Sarah Carter, Sylvia Van Kirk, and Jennifer Brown, began to challenge white-male bias in early fur trade documents, others, such as Newman in *The Company of Adventurers*, continued to rely on them uncritically. The problem with using HBC and JRAD uncritically is that such documents encourage the construction of stereotypic representations of Indigenous women, fostering dangerous cultural attitudes that condone violence. The numbers of missing and murdered Indigenous women in Canada are disturbing reminders of connections between easy squaw/whore stereotypes and dangerous cultural attitudes that condone violence and murder. Two cases that support this claim are the brutal rape and murder of Helen Betty Osbourne and the numerous rapes and murders of Indigenous women by serial killer John Crawford. Both cases revealed that the murderers believed Indigenous women were "easy squaws" who deserved violence done to them.

One has to wonder about the longevity of stereotypical representations of Indigenous women, particularly considering claims about the cross-cultural power of Indigenous women in work produced by Dr. Kim Anderson (Metis), Dr. Howard Adams (Metis), and Dr. Emma LaRocque (Metis). Anderson's *A Recognition of Being: Reconstructing Native Womanhood* acknowledges that historically, relative to their own cultures, Indigenous women exercised autonomy over their bodies and relations with others.[12] She devotes one chapter, "The Colonization of Native Womanhood," to how "Native women were understood and positioned in various traditional cultures ... briefly trac[ing] the changes that happened as a result of contact with Europeans."[13] She also makes it clear that although "Native womanhood" was dismantled over a long period of colonization at "different times for different peoples ... Native womanhood is not dead, but it has certainly been through a time of intense attack."[14] Adams's *Prison of Grass*[15] and LaRocque's *Defeathering the Indian*[16] provide historical contexts for the social, political, economic, and Spiritual conditions that altered ideological norms, which I read as shifting from gender-balanced cultures to white-eurocanadian-christian-patriarchal hierarchies. Adams and LaRocque are insightful and courageous scholars whose work challenged existing patriarchal colonial interpretations of history when it was not popular to do so: Adams provides a passionate and comprehensive discussion of the colonization of prairie Indigenous peoples, while LaRocque's astutely analyzes stereotypical representations of Native peoples. Together, Anderson, Adams, and LaRocque provide convincing evidence that connects literary representations of Indigenous people to white-eurocanadian-christian-patriarchal ideology and cultural attitudes. As I interpret their work, colonial institutions functioned as cultural destroyers intent on dis-membering signifying relations from cultural bodies.

In the 1800s in Canada, colonial laws were enacted through treaties and various legislative acts to eliminate Indigenous signifying female relations from cultural bodies. First of all, "Indian" and "half-breed" women were strategically segregated to small areas of land, called "Indian" reserves and "half-breed" colonies, where colonial agents could control them. Once dis-connected from their homelands, Indigenous women were encouraged to believe that their social, political, and economic disparity was peculiar and of their own creation. Adams claims that any development of a politi-cal nature or of consciousness was immediately repressed. To provide an example for such a claim, Adams compares outlawed empowering cere-monies and practices to those that posed no threat to the settlers' ideol-ogy.[17] His example calls to mind colonial strategies for dis-membering from Indigenous cultural bodies important female relations who functioned as creators, ceremonialists, headwomen, drummers, singers, clan mothers, medicine/Spiritual leaders, and political, social, and economic consultants.

Once subjected to colonization, Indigenous cultures were stripped of such influential female relations. Whereas some pre-colonial cultures encouraged social, political, and economic flexibility among genders, attempts were made after colonization to remove women from social, polit-ical, economic, and Spiritual processes. Whereas women once participated and contributed in meaningful ways as part of clan, tribal, and council con-sensus governments, under the colonial regime they were almost entirely excluded. The historical records of treaty negotiations, for example, reveal the blatant exclusion of women's participation, even though oral histories recall women's meaningful consultations. Indeed, the "Indian" headmen's signed X's on the various treaty documents confirms the whites' insistence on including only males in the negotiations process.

Once colonized, Indigenous people were to be dis-membered from cul-tural bodies and important signifying Indigenous female relations. In cultural practice, Indigenous women's freedom to exercise control over their bodies and relations with others was almost completely eradicated. Instead, their energies were channelled into less politically threatening activities, such as ladies' auxiliary groups, church rituals (marriage, bap-tism, confession, communion, confirmations, and funerals), and church-sponsored teas, bake sales, and bazaars. All Indigenous women's activities in the communities were, at least on the surface, completely controlled from birth until death by a white-christian patriarchy. Such ideological control was apparent in the organization of personal relations, the home, and community, in which women were strongly encouraged to adhere and

conform to patriarchy. To understand the strategic methods used to indoc-
trinate Indigenous women, one need only to turn to the christian-oper-
ated "Indian" residential schools and the "half-breed" day schools. In both
"Indian" and "half-breed" schools, women were primarily taught domestic
skills to prepare them for their future roles as "good" christian farm wives.
Women who demurred from the stringently imposed ideological norms
underlying the teachings were viewed as archaic squaws or promiscuous,
immoral, and scandalous women. While some women no doubt gave in
to the overwhelming pressures, others, like many of my female ancestors, chose to maintain their independence and autonomy. These women,
however, were subjected to ridicule, banishment, and alienation, and
eventually represented in stereotypic and derogatory bad "squaw" images.
Adams's retelling of a frightening ordeal with some Mounties who picked
him up on the highway outside his community is a reminder of prevailing sexist and racist attitudes during the 1950s through to the 1970s in
St. Louis, Saskatchewan. He claims that two Mounties used racism and
sexism to terrorize him: as they forcefully detained him, they spoke to
him of "halfbreed babes [who] liked to have their fun lying down ... [and
who] liked it better from a white man ... 'redskin hotboxes who didn't wear
any pants at all' ... [and who went] to bed with anyone for a beer."[18] In his
recollection of the Mounties and their comments, Adams appears somewhat perplexed by their fetishistic interest in "halfbreed" girls. He writes,
"They seemed to have an obsessive interest in native girls [although they
implied] ... that Metis girls were little more than sluts and too dirty for
Mounties."[19] Adams's recollection of the RCMP's comments and actions
reinforce my claim that signifying female relations were dis-membered
from Indigenous cultural bodies, and in their place stereotypes were used
to foster and then justify cultural attitudes.

Beatrice Culleton's *In Search of April Raintree* illustrates direct connections between literature, stereotypes, cultural attitudes, and resulting violence.[20] In her novel, Culleton creates the character Mrs. Semple (April
Raintree's social worker) to give voice to a stereotype she calls the "native
girl syndrome." According to Mrs. Semple, all Native girls inevitably become
pregnant, indulge in alcohol and drugs, engage in shoplifting and prostitution, end up in jail and on skid row, live with abusive men, and ultimately
live off society. While Culleton's Indigenous female characters reflect

feelings of powerlessness and oppression compounded with disillusion-ment and frustration, which encourage behaviours that sometimes appear to mirror stereotypes, her novel subverts the "native girl syndrome," the easy squaw, and to a much lesser extent the "Indian" princess by contextual-izing Indigenous women's lives in a social, political, and economic reality.

Read uncritically, how do stereotypes like the "native girl syndrome" from Culleton's *In Search of April Raintree*, "redskin hotboxes" from Adams's *Prison of Grass*, or Newman's "sluts—to satisfy the animal lust" from *Company of Adventurers* affect readers' cultural attitudes? In "Sexism and the Social Construction of Knowledge," Margaret Anderson explains that there is a very real relationship between images and reality, "either because images reflect social values ... or because images create social ide-als upon which people model their behaviour and attitudes."[21] Anderson further explains that "images are produced by working people; even if we see them as social myths, they are connected to the social systems in which they are created."[22] Thiong'o reasons that while many people naively look upon literature as merely belonging to a surreal or metaphysical realm, literary creations powerfully shape our attitudes and beliefs towards life. Thiong'o convincingly argues that

> the product of a writer's pen both reflects reality and also attempts to persuade us to take a certain attitude to that reality. The persuasion can be a direct appeal on behalf of a writer's open doctrine or it can be an indirect appeal through "influencing the imagination, feelings, and actions of the recipient" in a certain way toward certain goals and a set of values, consciously or unconsciously held.[23]

In his examination of literature and colonization, Thiong'o connects liter-ary texts to systems of oppression and genocide. He describes literature as a subtle weapon that "works through influencing emotions, the imagi-nation, and the consciousness of a people."[24] The western ruling classes reflected themselves, their images, and their history in the literature (as Newman's representations of Indigenous women illustrate), while the colonized saw only "distorted image[s] of themselves and of their his-tory" in the colonizer's constructions.[25] Like Thiong'o, Adams connects literature, stereotypes, and cultural attitudes to both school and literature when he describes Native children who enter school "surrounded with white-supremacist ideas and stories—every image glorify[ing] white success."[26] He also reveals connections between imperialism, colonization, and white-christian patriarchy, which "became woven into Canadian institutions such as the church, the schools, and the courts, and it has remained the working ideology of these institutions."[27] As both Adams and Culleton reveal in their representations of police and social workers, Native people "cannot avoid seeing the cultural images and symbols of white supremacy, because they are everywhere in society, especially in movies, television, comic books, and textbooks."[28] Joan Rockwell refers to the universal existence of censorship to show how what we read does affect us. In fact, she concludes that policy makers must believe that what we read (even when fictionalized) "may have some potentially dangerous influence on people's beliefs, and consequently (possibly) on their social behaviour."[29] The voices of the mounties documented in Adams's *Prison of Grass* and the social worker (Mrs. Semple) from Culleton's *April Raintree* are reminders of the prevalence of white supremacy in 1960s–1980s Canadian society.

As the writers cited in this chapter make clear, there are very real connections between literature, stereotypes, and cultural attitudes. Thus, it is my contention that one cannot read literature as merely finely crafted words preserved over time in poems, essays, short stories, and novels considered to be the best of a particular era. Writers such as Dumont, Thiong'o, Berkhofer, Stedman, Maeser-Lemieux, Newman, Anderson (Kim), Adams, LaRocque, Culleton, Anderson (Margaret), and Rockwell connect literature to an art that powerfully, politically, and persuasively influences uncritical readers. And, as this chapter has made attempts to show, because early Canadian literature absorbed and conformed to the developing nation's political and nationalistic agenda in varying degrees, it manifested the dominant white-eurocanadian-christian patriarchy's economic, philosophic, religious, and political codes and conventions. Thus, without critical attention to its white-euro-christian-patriarchal ideological centre, Canadian literature (as an expression of the nation's prevailing ideological structures) will continue to function as a cultural destroyer that dis-members from Indigenous cultural bodies important signifying female relations. An example supporting this conclusion is the practice of calling Koochums "grandmothers." When I am introduced to my granddaughters' friends and family, speakers impose "grandmother" as a term of reference even after I name myself their "Coco." Contemporary literature is filled with these kinds of imposed references for signifying female relations.

Moreover, without powerful, political, and persuasive Indigenous female literary creators (such as those cited throughout this chapter), literary texts constructed outside Indigenous ideological paradigms will continue to function as cultural destroyers of important signifying female relations, imprisoning women in stereotypes that obscure and distort our very real and lived experiences. Throughout the Americas, powerful, political, and persuasive Indigenous female literary creators have infused their texts with representations of empowering female deities, Spirits, and roles. For example, Paula Gunn Allen's (Pueblo Laguna Sioux) *The Sacred Hoop, Spider Woman's Granddaughters*, and *Grandmothers of the Light* include representations of empowering mythological female deities and superhuman Spirits.[30] Marla Powers's (Oglala) "Sex Roles and Social Structures" includes empowering representations of White Buffalo Calf Woman, who, according to the author, represents Lakota culture and all humanity, and who brought the sacred pipe and rituals for living a good and balanced life with all the relations.[31] Native American anthropologist Dr. Beatrice Medicine's (Sioux) "Warrior Woman— Sex Role Alternatives for Plains Indian Women" enriches her text with varying cross-cultural empowering roles for women among the Lakota, Navajo, Blackfoot, Kutenai, Tlingit, Ottawa, Peigan, Gras Ventres, and Cheyenne cultures.[32] In particular, she includes in her work warrior women whose roles challenge prevailing myths about Indigenous women. Lorraine Littlefield's "Women Traders in the Maritime Fur Trade"[33] also includes cross-cultural roles of Indigenous women as traders, fishers, and hunters among the Haida, Nootka, Tlingit, and Tsimshian. Priscilla Buffalohead's (Anishinaabe) "Farmers Warriors Traders: A Fresh Look at Ojibway Women,"[34] as the title suggests, infuses her text with empowering roles for Ojibway women as farmers, warriors, and traders. Portraying varying roles of Indigenous women cross-culturally, as revealed in the work of Gunn Allen, Powers, Medicine, Littlefield, and Buffalohead, encourages us to re-member ourselves to culture-specific bodies and important female relations who provide numerous possibilities for constituting Being. Whereas the scholarship included in the original manuscript for *Iskwewak* had to be culled from limited sources, there are now numerous culturally specific bodies of work revealing Indigenous women as very important signifying creators, mythological and superhuman beings, political leaders, ceremonialists, negotiators, traders, trappers, farmers, and warriors (some of which are cited in the revised bibliography). Without such scholarly work, the body of Canadian literature will continue to encourage ideological confirmation to the so-called book of god, wherein social ordering is premised on a powerfully protected god-king-man-boy-woman-girl hierarchy. Unchallenged by Great-Spirited Indigenous female creators, literature as an ideological apparatus connected to christian dogmatic traditions will continue to represent women as merely appendages to men. Left unchallenged by writers who re-member themselves to signifying female relations, the literature will encourage dangerous cultural attitudes that condone violence against Indigenous women.

Photo by Patrick McCloski, from work on script development at Wanuskewin International Heritage Park.

CHAPTER THREE

Keeping the Fire: Iskwewak Kah' Ki Yaw Ni Wahkomakanak

It had taken months for all the songs, protocol, and ceremony to be learned. Many of the oldest songs and ceremonies had been forgotten ... vanquished by the missionaries years ago, so now what had once been 'common knowledge' had to be recalled from other reservations, books, and memories of the oldest people.

—Winona LaDuke, *Last Standing Woman*

Between the 1970s and 1980s in Canada, emergent voices of Indigenous women writers such as Maria Campbell, Emma LaRocque, Lee Maracle, Lenore Keeshig-Tobias, Jeannette Armstrong, and Beatrice Culleton began to challenge stereotypical representations of Indigenous women that perpetuated colonization, racism, and sexism. Their work disrupted the minefield of stereotypes that falsified reality and suggested subliminally that we are sexually promiscuous, Indian princesses, squaw drudges, suffering helpless victims, and tawny temptresses. Prior to the collected works of such writers, sexually promiscuous, princess, squaw, victim, and temptress stereotypes too frequently appeared on the pages of books, fomenting cultural attitudes that justified sexual, physical, verbal, or psychological violence against Indigenous women. While their work continues to challenge colonization, racism, and sexism, the stereotypes remain deeply entrenched because they are part of a Canadian mainstream ideological system that I connect to white-christian patriarchy/matriarchy. Moreover, the violence against Indigenous women continues, in part, because we have to find strategies for moving beyond words.

Connected to the colonial agenda, 20th-century eurocanadian literature perpetuated stereotypes of Indigenous women to justify colonization and condone racism and sexism. In my efforts to understand the colonial mindset, I turn to Algerian psychiatrist Frantz Fanon's *The Wretched of the Earth*.[1] Although his theorizing is dated and based primarily on African experiences, I consider his work useful and relevant to contemporary North American Indigenous contexts. Fanon claims that European colonizers used a divide-and-conquer strategy for disempowering "natives" and maintaining control. According to the Algerian psychiatrist, Europeans "multiplied divisions and opposing groups ... fashioned classes and sometimes even racial prejudices ... and endeavoured by every means to bring about and intensify the stratification of colonized societies."[2] He also claims that after "natives" were strategically disconnected from their source of power, the colonizer substituted images of the "natives" as quintessentially and absolutely evil. Such images, when applied to women, suggested that they were also "insensible to ethics [and] ... the enemy of values," and therefore in need of christianization and colonization. Accordingly, colonizers created justifications for dismembering important female relations from cultural bodies and erasing all Indigenous traditions and cultures, and replacing "native" languages with their own.[3] Images such as the romantic Indian princess, the easy squaw, and the hopeless, suffering victim became useful constructs for justifying christianization and colonization.

In my reading of R. G. Thwaites's *Jesuit Relations and Allied Documents* (JRAD),[4] I concluded that most christian missionaries were misogynists who employed coercive, manipulative, and even sadistic strategies (I read the Jesuit and Oblate missionary documents in preparation for my Native Studies honours degree on the Cowessess Indian Residential School). The Jesuits were part of the colonial strategy to remove "Indians" from the land, and their letters to the home office, compiled in the JRAD, reveal such strategies in their attempts to convert Spiritually and physically weakened human beings. I was particularly astounded to find conversion strategies employed by so-called men of god, and even more so, their propaganda-like letters encouraging readers to believe that Indigenous people en masse naively abandoned their own Spiritual/medicine specialists, many of them women. An untrained or uncritical pair of eyes may very well read colonial documents such as the JRAD as evidence that Indigenous people, particularly women, willingly handed over power and accepted christian patriarchy. Logically, it just doesn't make sense.

My readings of Eleanor Leacock's "Montagnais Women and the Jesuit Program for Colonization," Priscilla Buffalohead's "Farmers Warriors Traders: A Fresh Look At Ojibway Women," Patricia Albers's "New Perspectives on Plains Indian Women," and Osennontion/Marlyn Kane's "Our World: According to Osennontion and Skonaganleh: ra" encourage re-examinations of old colonial documents and old truths. Starting from the premise that there are significant interpretive contradictions in much of the scholarly work on old colonial documents such as the JRAD, the collective writings of Leacock, Buffalohead, Albers, and Osennontion encourage re-readings from a non-sexist and non-racist decolonizing agenda. Leacock describes male authors of some of the old documents as "European observers who did not know personally the people about whom they were writing."[5] Accordingly, those authors represented "Indian" women as slaves.[6] Leacock then describes "a man who knew the Montagnais-Naskapi well," and therefore he described women as controlling their own work and making decisions autonomously.[7] Like Leacock, Buffalohead uncovered some surviving documents from the mid-17th to the early 20th century, written by French, British, and American colonists, which reveal considerable bias and contradictory images of Indigenous women.[8] In her re-reading, she offered interpretations of the documents that presented Indigenous women as dynamic and resourceful producers/practitioners of culture. Thus, while much of the late 20th-century scholarship reproduced christian-male-biased readings concluding that missionaries acting as colonial agents successfully dis-membered from cultural bodies all important female relations, Albers and Osennontion/Marlyn Kane illustrate new interpretive approaches to old documents that require re-examinations of old truths. In her study of Plains "Indian" women, Albers claims that the Plains "Indian" is the quintessential symbol of "Indianness" for the majority of Americans and Europeans, and her work reveals that it is "the male-dominated universe of native diplomacy, warfare, and hunting that has captured the attention of national image makers."[9] Thus, she concludes that the male-dominated eurocentric view of the "Indian" or the "Native" has almost totally effaced from history Indigenous women. The word *almost* is extremely relevant to understanding the survival of Indigenous female relations, given the power and might of colonial christian patriarchy. A former president of the Native Women's Association of Canada, Osennontion/Kane calls for a re-examination of old truths.[10] Like Albers, Osennontion's re-examination of old truths necessarily involves deconstructing stereotypical representations of Indigenous women that uphold colonization, promote racism, and justify sexism. As I interpret their work, a re-examination of old truths in the revisiting of old texts helps us to re-member important female relations for constituting healthy and wholesome Beings. Until such a time, racist and sexist stereotypes will, according to Albers, obscure fundamental realities of Indigenous women.[11]

Deconstructing from Canadian literature the Indian princess, easy squaw, and suffering helpless victim stereotypes may feel overwhelming and challenging. Deconstruction projects seem overwhelming and challenging because the stereotypes are firmly planted in age-old christian patriarchal power structures that few have the strength of Spirit to challenge. Also, deconstructing stereotypes of Indigenous women feels overwhelming and challenging because the projects require not only subverting racist and sexist assumptions carried by colonial and patriarchal discourse in English, but also re-creating, renaming, and re-membering signifying relations. Perhaps the most challenging work for us as Indigenous women is re-creating, renaming, and re-membering ourselves to signifying female relations in stories written in English. In addition to long-term strategic efforts to dis-member important female relations from cultural bodies, policies were developed to eliminate Indigenous languages: indeed, our languages, cultures, and relations have been violently traumatized through programmed and controlled terrorism during the colonial era. And, as my 23 years of teaching English to Indigenous students reveals, many contemporary Indigenous peoples have a disconcerting relationship with the English language as a result of "Indian" residential schools.

My re-reading of selected 20th-century history reveals "Indian" residential schools to be "indoctrination camps" that used programmed terrorism to dis-member signifying female relations from cultural bodies.
Jeannette Armstrong astutely describes residential schools as camps of
indoctrination that effectively employed church dogma, education strategies, state policies, legalized kidnapping, and imprisonment of "Indian"
children to kill cultural bodies.[12] In these places of indoctrination, biblical
stories and primary readers were used as tools to impose christian dogma
and dis-member Indigenous female relations from cultural bodies. In
residential schools, the English language became a tool of indoctrination,
which LaRocque claims for a "Native woman ... is like an ideological onion
whose stinging layers of racism and sexism must be peeled away."[13] Thus,
as it was used in residential schools, the English of biblical stories and
primary readers became a tool for programmed terrorism to effect ideological changes.

Tomson Highway's *Dry Lips Oughta Move to Kapuskasing*[14] and Richard
Wagamese's *Indian Horse*[15] are two contemporary fictional stories that
shine a light on the brutal methods used to christianize and colonize
"Indians." Highway's *Dry Lips* lights up the complex dynamics of imposed
christianity. In this play, Highway effectively employs symbols of both
christianity and "Indian" Spirituality: he uses the crucifix as a symbol
of christianity and Nanabush/Patsy Pegahmahgahbow as a symbol of
"Indian" Spirituality. Notably, feminist (both Indigenous and non-Indigenous) critics took issue with Highway's representation of a brutal rape
scene, although it symbolically represented christianity's brutal rape of
female-centred Indigenous Spirituality. To convey such brutality, Highway
employed the crucifix as a tool of rape and a young "Indian" boy suffering from fetal alcohol syndrome as the perpetrator who raped Nanabush/
Patsy Pegahmahgahbow. Like Highway's *Dry Lips*, Wagamese's *Indian
Horse* sheds light on the brutality of christianity and colonization. His
text also provides numerous examples of strategic programmed terrorism in the fictional St. Jerome's "Indian" residential school. Wagamese's
novel describes strategies of programmed terrorism through the eyes of
his protagonist, Saul Indian Horse. A young and vulnerable Anishinaabe,
Saul witnessed terrorized "boys and girls [who died] standing on their own

two feet ... runaways carried back, frozen solid as boards ... bodies hung from rafters on thin ropes ... wrists slashed and the cascade of blood on the bathroom floor and, one time, a young boy impaled on the tines of a pitchfork that he'd shoved through himself."[16] Saul remembers, too, watching a young girl so terrorized that she "calmly fill[ed] the pockets of her apron with rocks and walk[ed] away across the field" to a creek where she "sat on the bottom and drowned."[17] As Saul witnesses such programmed terrorism at St. Gerome's residential school, he's convinced that acts of self-torture "would never stop, never change, so long as that school stood ... [and] as long as they continued to pull kids from the bush and from the arms of their people."[18] And, while Wagamese seems to suggest in his killing off of the archetypal Naomi that important female relations have been forever dis-membered from Indigenous cultural bodies, his description of the Creator as "she" re-members Great-Spirited signifying female relations to the Anishinaabe cultural body.[19]

Prior to "Indian" residential schools, christian conversions, and colonization, Indigenous peoples relied on narrative memories and oral stories that, among many other things, re-membered us to signifying female relations. In my culture-specific ceremonies, all signifying relations (including women) are represented in the phrase *Kah' Ki Yaw Ni Wahkomakanak*. As well, in my Treaty #4 homeland, Kah' Ki Yaw Ni Wahkomakanak/signifying relations transmit in conversations a culture-specific Spirituality and philosophy. In books written in English, a comparable "all my relations" expression, according to Thomas King's (Cherokee-Greek) *All My Relations: An Anthology of Contemporary Canadian Fiction*, reminds us philosophically about who we are.[20] As I interpret King's words, the "all my relations" philosophy connects Being to relations beyond our human existence. Accordingly, the "all my relations" philosophy encourages respectful and harmonious relations with all of Creation, both female and male human relations, Spiritual relations, and other than human relations. A philosophical expression of Indigenous Spirituality, "all my relations" signifies both the solidarity of Indigenous peoples throughout the world and a continuity of Indigenous women's power. An "all my relations" philosophy signifies solidarity with Indigenous peoples throughout the world because we share a Spiritual relationship to land, symbolically represented as Mother Earth. The Independent Commission of International Humanitarian Issues[21] as well as the more recent United Nations Declaration on the Rights of Indigenous Peoples[22] acknowledge our shared world views that signify custodial concepts of the land and its natural resources. And, in its formation in 1975, the World Council of Indigenous Peoples institutionalized an "all my relations–like" common ideology, thereby formally acknowledging the solidarity of Indigenous peoples throughout the world. The "all my relations" philosophy, represented by Indigenous keepers of knowledge in ceremonies and books written in English that express Spirituality, lights up the continuity of Indigenous women's signifying relational power.

During the writing of my doctoral dissertation, I was frustrated because I could not call up from memory a word that acknowledges Indigenous women's Great-Spirited powers, which I hear acknowledged in ceremonies. Anishinaabe ceremonialist and Bear Clan Keeper of Knowledge Elder Dan Musqua assured me there is such a word, and then he presented me with the word *Manitoukwe*.[23] As I understand them, the words *all my relations* and *Manitoukwe* acknowledge the enduring signifying relational powers of women. In fact, I interpret the word *Manitoukwe* as a signifier of Indigenous women's creative powers. However, while some Indigenous languages and ceremonies refer to women as Creators scholarly attention to such ways of thinking is sorely lacking. I connect the lack of scholarship to bell hooks's *Talking Back,* in which she claims that silence is often misinterpreted as the appropriate response of women or as a sign of "woman's submission to patriarchal authority."[24] I also connect the lack of scholarship about Indigenous female relations being Creators to her references to "crucial differences" between WASP and Black women in the United States and Canada. When hooks points out that Black women have not been silent, I am reminded of LaRocque's insistence that Indigenous women have not been silent, that in fact our voices were suppressed by publishers who were "influenced by uncomprehending critics and audiences ... [and therefore] controlled the type of material that was published."[25]

Historically, I can understand the lack of scholarship and literature acknowledging the creative and Spiritual attributes of Indigenous women. Instead of encouraging Indigenous women to articulate in written

English our very real lives and influences, publishers of books during the last quarter of the 20th century in Canada encouraged non-Indigenous writers to write for us, and those kinds of publications privileged a white idealism. Instead of acknowledging the Manitoukwe-like voices of Emma LaRocque, Beatrice Culleton, Lee Maracle, Jeannette Armstrong, Beth Cuthand, Lenore Keeshig Tobias, Louise Halfe, Marie Annharte Baker, Maria Campbell, and others, publishers (initially) ignored or dismissed their work. Strong autonomous representations of Great-Spirited women created by equally powerful Indigenous women writers were therefore undermined by stereotypes that fit white supremacist ideas of women. In his groundbreaking critique of colonization in *Prison of Grass*, Dr. Howard Adams theorizes that white idealism became a standard synonymous with goodness, purity, and virtue. For women, white idealism meant "flowing golden hair ... [a] lovely white face ... pale skin, thin lips, and gorgeous big blue eyes."[26] Not surprisingly, most Indigenous women did not fit white ideals and, therefore, they became undesirable and associated with oppression. This "white ideal," as he describes it, is symptomatic of the colonial mindset and cultural attitudes that reduce Indigenous women to stereotypes rather than uphold realistic and positive images. So, even though writers such as LaRocque, Campbell, Maracle, Culleton, and others were creating and producing work that represented Indigenous women as survivors of economic and political oppression, publishers dismissed their work as "biased" and "bitter." LaRocque reasons that "our anger, legitimate as it was and is, was exaggerated as 'militant' and used as an excuse not to hear us. There was little comprehension of an articulate anger reflecting an awakening and a call to liberation, not a psychological problem to be defused in a therapist's room."[27] Dismissing Indigenous women as important female creators and producers by using words such as *biased* and *bitter* was one of many strategies used by publishers of Canadian literature.

Another method to suppress the Great-Spirited voices of Indigenous women was to use one person's life as representative of a whole culture. For example, while Maria Campbell's fictionalized autobiography[28] established possibilities for new literary productions by revising and redefining Indigenous women's culture-specific experiences, *Halfbreed* was reduced to "grist for social workers" intent on lumping all women into a big, brown blob of nativeness.[29] And, while some may claim that Campbell's book feeds readers' appetites for squaw drudge, sexually promiscuous whore, and helpless victim stereotypes, I would argue that her book is important still because it encourages re-readings of Indigenous women's lives. In fact, if Campbell's story is re-examined from the perspective encouraged by feminist writer Adrienne Rich, that is, "of looking back, of seeing with fresh eyes, of entering an old text from a new critical direction,"[30] readers may come to understand Indigenous women as enormously powerful Creators.

Campbell's *Halfbreed* is also still an important book because it employs writing in English as a strategy for deconstructing from Canadian literature's racist and sexist stereotypes of Indigenous women. Anthologist Connie Fife encourages Indigenous women to take control of the language when she writes, "The written word does not have to be wrapped in the thoughts of the colonizers, but rather can convey the resilience of our survival."[31] Strategically, more and more Indigenous women are using the English language to challenge racism and sexism, articulate survival, re-member relations, renew cultural bodies, and preserve Indigenous knowledge. Following Campbell's pioneering work, Indigenous women began using the English language to talk back to colonial christian patriarchy. In fact, I read books such as Marilyn Dumont's *A Really Good Brown Girl*; editors Joy Harjo's and Gloria Bird's *Reinventing the Enemy's Language: Contemporary Native Women's Writings of North America*; Lee Maracle's *Bobby Lee: Indian Rebel*, *I Am Woman*, and *Sojourner's Truth*; Emma LaRocque's *Defeathering the Indian;* Marie Annharte Baker's *Being on the Moon;* Jeannette Armstrong's *Slash*; Louise Erdrich's *Love Medicine, The Beet Queen*, and *Tracks*; Mary Crow Dog's *Lakota Woman* (co-authored by Richard Erdoes); Agnes Grant's *Our Bit of Truth*; the contemporary western Canadian "Native" women's anthology *Writing the Circle*; Louise Halfe's *Bear Bones & Feathers*; Beth Cuthand's *Voices in the Waterfall*, and editor Connie Fife's *The Colour of Resistance: A Contemporary Collection of Writing by Aboriginal Women*, and others as created by Great-Spirited Indigenous women whose work reveals imaginative possibilities for constituting Being within culture-specific bodies.[32]

Their work, as well as the enormous bodies of work produced by Indigenous women within the first decade of the new millennium, is proof that Great Spirited female relations have not been completely dis-membered from Indigenous cultural bodies. Indeed, our voices have kept alive the sanctity and creative power of maternal lineages thousands of years old. Prior to the colonization of the Americas, most Indigenous cul-tures acknowledged the importance of maternal lineages by promoting gender-balanced relations with all of Creation. Paula Gunn Allen claims that colonial strategies to conquer Indigenous peoples were doomed to fail because women were both powerful and influential.[33] Thus, agents of white-eurocanadian patriarchy—represented throughout history as explor-ers/merchants, colonial government officials, and christian missionar-ies—created economic, political, and Spiritual strategies to dis-member important female relations from cultural bodies. Despite such attempts to usurp Indigenous women's power, some contemporary cultural practices and political actions mirror—cross-culturally—self-governing and self-determining women. In 1971 and 1977, respectively, Jeannette Corbiere-Lavell (Anishinaabe) and Sandra Lovelace (Maliseet) legally challenged the Indian Act's discriminatory policy towards "Indian" women. Prior to their legal challenges of the Indian Act and the subsequent 1985 Canadian Charter of Rights and Freedoms, "Indian" women (including myself) who married non-"Indian" men lost their legal rights as "Indians" and thus became "non-status Indians," while "non-Indian" women who married "Indian" men became legal "Indian" women. In 1991, Kanine' Keha: Ka (Mohawk) women courageously defended the people and their ancestral homeland, maintained peace, and negotiated with the Canadian army during the standoff at Oka, Quebec. Their actions were later represented in film by an equally courageous and autonomous filmmaker, Alanis Obomsawin (Abenaki), in *Kanehsatake: 270 Years of Resistance*.[34] In 1991 and again in 1994, a cross-cultural council of women Elders raised up into office Ovide Mercredi, the newly elected national chief of the Assembly of First Nations. In 1999, Vicky Scrimbitt (Anishinaabe-Metis-Nehiowe) successfully challenged the Sakimay First Nation's unjust treatment of "Bill C-31 women," resulting in "a landmark decision that could have far-reaching implications for First Nations across Canada. [Indeed], a Federal

Court judge has determined that a Saskatchewan Indian band broke the law by denying one of its [female] members the right to cast a ballot in band elections."[35] Amid the epidemic of violence and serial killings of Indigenous women in Canada, too, Metis filmmaker Christine Welsh's *Finding Dawn*[36] pioneered work in the field of missing and murdered women. In fact, we have a good many Indigenous pioneering women in Saskatchewan, such as Darlene Okemaysim-Sicotte (Cree)—the co-chair of Iskwewuk E-wichiwitochik (Women Walking Together)—as well as Nina Wilson, Sylvia McAdam, and Jessica Gordon, who, along with non-Indigenous ally Sheela McLean, inspired the global Idle No More Movement. The same year, in support of the Idle No More Movement, Chief Theresa Spence (Cree) selflessly gave up personal comforts when she employed Ghandi-like political strategies by fasting to call attention to Bill C-45: her self-determining actions and strength brought worldwide attention to the struggles of Indigenous peoples in Canada. Despite very real demonstrations of Indigenous women's power such as those cited above, both the white-eurocanadian-christian patriarchy and now the Indigenous patriarchy continue to represent Indigenous women in racist and sexist stereotypes that promote negative cultural attitudes, as has been evident in media representations of Pam Palmater, an educated, outspoken, and media-savvy Mi'Kmaw lawyer, professor, and political activist. Another example of racist and sexist stereotypes imposed on powerful women is when the first female vice-chief of the Federation of Saskatchewan Indian Nations (FSIN) was sworn into office. As the vice-chief was being honoured with the traditional blanket, she was told by one of the FSIN representatives, "this is not a snagging blanket." This was even more offensive because I was watching the induction ceremony with my Aboriginal Women in Canada class, who understood "snagging blanket" to be a sexual innuendo. As the growing numbers of missing and murdered Indigenous women in Canada reveal, violence against Indigenous women—which feeds off of racist and sexist stereotypes—has reached epidemic proportions. While I acknowledge the political efforts of communities, organizations, and individuals to develop strategies for missing and murdered Indigenous women in Canada, I firmly believe that the violence epidemic will not be eradicated without serious attention and action towards the psychosis that feeds it and the cultural attitudes that condone it. It is my sincere hope that this book will in some small way stimulate readers to develop strategies for moving beyond words.

This was a very sad moment during an interview with Christine Welsh for the film *Finding Dawn* as I shared memories of witnessing my mother being raped. Photo credit: Banchu Hanuse.

CHAPTER FOUR

Stereotypes and Dis-membered Relations

Betty, if I start to write a poem about you
it might turn out to be
about hunting season instead
about "open season" on native women
it might turn out to be
about your face young and hopeful
staring back at me hollow now
from a black and white page
it might be about the "townsfolk" (gentle word)
townsfolk who "believed native girls were easy"
and "less likely to complain if a sexual proposition led to violence."
—Marilyn Dumont, "Helen Betty Osborne"

In the early morning hours of November 13, 1971, Helen Betty Osborne was grabbed off the street, forced into a car, and murdered by four white men intent on finding "an Indian girl with whom to drink and have sex."[1] Before her death, Osborne was brutally beaten and sexually assaulted. On her young body, the autopsy observed 50 stab wounds, a smashed skull, broken cheekbones and palate, damaged lungs, and torn kidneys. Trial evidence also revealed that "a screw driver was at least one weapon used" and that other weapons were used, "presumably hands or feet or some other blunt instrument."[2] The *Report of the Aboriginal Inquiry of Manitoba* later concluded that Helen Betty Osborne

> fell victim to vicious stereotypes born of ignorance and aggression when she was picked up by four drunken men looking for sex. Her attackers seemed to be operating on the assumption that Aboriginal women were promiscuous and open to enticement through alcohol or violence. It is evident that the men who abducted Osborne believed that young Aboriginal women were objects with no human value beyond sexual gratification.[3]

Like the missing and murdered Indigenous women in 2015 in Canada, Helen Betty Osborne was a valued human being. Considered together, they all had cultural and familial relations with grandmothers, mothers, granddaughters, daughters, sisters, cousins, and aunties. Yet, as in the case of Osborne, increasing numbers of Indigenous women (myself included) continue to be viewed as having no human value. University of Manitoba professor Dr. Emma LaRocque makes it very clear that "the image of the sexually loose 'squaw' renders all Native girls and women vulnerable to gross sexual, physical and/or verbal violence."[4] In her beautifully and poetically crafted essay "Tides, Towns and Trains," LaRocque admits that she does not feel safe "to walk our streets, to ride in taxis or trains, to go to a hospital or to meet a police officer alone."[5] And, the *Report of the Aboriginal Justice Inquiry of Manitoba* specifically connects stereotypic images—as standardized visual pictures, held in common by members of a group, that represent an oversimplified picture of another group—to cultural attitudes that condone violence against Indigenous women.

Historically, as previous chapters have shown, Indigenous women have been grossly misrepresented, primarily by male historians, missionaries, and writers whose ideological foundation privileges and values men over women, and white women over women of colour. In other words, stereotypes are constructed from within a patriarchal hierarchy that represents women somewhere between good and bad, or between madonna and whore. Marlene Nourbese Philip (Trinidadian–Black-Canadian) connects such stereotypes to literature, claiming that "traditionally, the unfettered nature of the imagination" of men in the arts conformed to "patriarchal visions of women."[6] She also reasons that "in a racist, sexist, classist society, the imagination, if left unexamined, can and does serve the ruling class of the time."[7] Thus, she concludes that it is dangerous for non-Indigenous writers to move into other cultures, particularly "the Native Canadian culture which theirs has oppressed and exploited," because "without careful thought, they are likely to perpetuate stereotypical and one dimensional views of that culture."[8] The discussion ahead considers Nourbese Philip's claim, reasoning, and conclusion to shed light on two celebrated Canadian writers, William Patrick Kinsella and Margaret Laurence. Using Nourbese Philip's claim, reasoning, and conclusion, the discussion connects Kinsella and Laurence to writers who drew on selected stereotypes from the oppressed and exploited "Native Canadian culture" in their representations of Indigenous women. While both writers have produced a considerable body of work, this chapter turns to Kinsella's "Linda Star"[9] and Laurence's "The Loons,"[10] two short stories that portray Indigenous women in stereotypical representations that foster negative cultural attitudes and condone violence against women.

A general review of their collective body of works and relative criticism, however, may lead some to conclude that Kinsella and Laurence are incomparable writers. Certainly, some readers and critics are of the view that Kinsella exhibits no social consciousness when he exploits "Indian" peoples' misery, or that he fails to provide a social, political, or economic context for the miserable conditions in which he sets his "Indian" characters. Readers and critics may therefore come to believe that what plagues real "Indian" communities is of our own creation, that we are burdensome to hardworking and honest taxpayers. Wider read than the average readers, literary critics view Kinsella's representations of Indigenous people with mixed reactions: some suggest that his representative images are sympathetic and positive, while others identify them as problematic. Gordon Johnston describes an "ambivalent and uneasy response of many to the Indians" in Kinsella's work.[11] For Johnson, Kinsella's stories fail to provide closure and "the effect is of destabilized expectations and reactions; [thus] we have no final sense of how funny or how disturbing a story is."[12] Johnson concludes, therefore, that "what seems tragic in one context will seem hilarious in another, and we struggle uncomfortably with morally ambivalent events."[13] Eli Mandel describes representations of Indigenous people constructed by both Kinsella and Laurence as "sympathetic to the Native."[14]

Some readers and critics have described Laurence as creating fiction (relative to the period in which she was writing) compassionately and with an understanding of the complex issues of classism and racism. Most eurocanadian literary critics view Laurence's representations of Indigenous people as positive and sympathetic portrayals, specifically her Metis characters. In "Prairie Writers and the Metis: Rudy Wiebe and Margaret Laurence," George Woodcock claims that the Metis in Laurence's work "are not introduced merely to heighten the local colour of the prairie setting ... [but because they] play important roles in affecting the attitudes, the actions and even the fates of the people involved with them."[15] Angelika Maeser-Lemieux interprets the Metis in Laurence's work as "metaphor for the alienated and repressed part of the individual and collective psyche in patriarchal culture."[16] She reads Laurence's Metis characters, too, as heighteners of consciousness, incorporating European and Indigenous worlds and therefore mediating "the archaic element in the psyche and culture to the heroine."[17] Accordingly, Maeser-Lemieux concludes that Laurence's Metis embody an unconscious "primordial image," "which compensates for the one-sidedness of the conscious outlook of the prevailing cultural norm."[18]

My analysis of the collective works and relative criticism of Laurence and Kinsella reveals them to be highly effective writers whose stories significantly influence readers' beliefs about and attitudes towards Indigenous women. I chose in the original text to selectively review the work of Laurence and Kinsella because they are extremely popular Canadian writers whose work continues to influence the world community. My own analyses leave me to conclude that the Indigenous women portrayed in Kinsella's "Linda Star" and Laurence's "The Loons" are related to the body of stereotypes that represent us as creatures of nature, tawny temptresses, femme fatales, Indian princesses, easy squaws, and suffering, helpless victims. In his short story, Kinsella represents Linda Star as a demoralized and promiscuous "Indian" woman, an easy squaw-like whore who falls prey to inherent weaknesses. Indeed, for Kinsella, Linda Star is not merely a woman gone bad; she is inherently bad. Comparably, Laurence represents the Metis girl Piquette Tonnerre as epitomizing most of the stereotypic images of Indigenous women generated and reproduced by eurocanadian culture. Both stories employ stereotypes of Indigenous women that foster cultural attitudes and affect the way Canadian society relates to us. For, as the *Report of the Aboriginal Justice Inquiry of Manitoba* concludes, stereotypical images of Indigenous women encourage views held in common by many Canadians that we have no human value beyond sexual gratification.

As a widely read Nehiowe-Metis-Anishinaabekwe reader and literary critic of Indigenous literatures, I view Kinsella's constructions of Indigenous women as fostering dangerous cultural attitudes that legitimize violence and abuse of Indigenous women. In his book *Dance Me Outside*, he loads his text with violence and abuse directed towards Indigenous women. In "Illianna Comes Home," Kinsella's Eathen Firstrider "polishes the big blade of his hunting knife ... and talks about taking scalps" in anticipation of Illianna's (and the white man she has married) return home.[19] He also loads his short story "Dance Me Outside" with violence and abuse directed towards Indigenous women: in this story, he writes about some white guys who cut Little Margaret Wolfchild's belly open "with a knife and sort of stuffed her body in a garbage can."[20] The events represented in this particular story frighteningly parallel the Osborne case. For example, both Helen Betty Osborne and Little Margaret Wolfchild were viciously and brutally murdered. And, in both cases, Osborne's and Wolfchild's killers escaped justice. And, perhaps most compelling, in both Osbourne's and Wolfchild's cases, the Canadian justice system failed them.

In "Linda Star," the short story under review here, Kinsella places Linda Star in an apparent plot set against Calgary street life, but the subplot reflects the author's own white-christian idealism. On Calgary's downtown skid row, he places Linda Star in a relationship with Silas Ermineskin, a sort of backwoods reserve boy who comes to the big city with equally big dreams. Kinsella characterizes Linda as a fast-talking hooker whose pimp, protector, and sometimes lover is a rude and arrogant whiteman named Clifton Black. Although Kinsella's plot foregrounds Calgary street life and relative street ideals, the story implicitly promotes the author's white-christian idealism in his representations of characters and plotted events. In other words, Kinsella promotes a white-christian ideal by foregrounding the street people's values and then ultimately judging those values against his own white-christian idealism. For example, Linda Star is described as a girl who smiles at Silas "real nice but real bold."[21] The implication here is that there is an appropriate and acceptable way of smiling, perhaps reserved for good/respectable women. Similarly, Kinsella describes Linda as a competent, no less than $100-a-day, hooker. However, his description of Linda as a savvy hooker conflicts with subsequent descriptions of her dreams of marriage, babies, and a chicken farm. In fact, Linda's marriage, baby, and chicken farm dreams seem to be Kinsella's covert promotion of a white (picket fence) idealism. It is interesting, too, that Kinsella represents Linda as Silas's second choice, a kind of "Indian" companion in the fur trade tradition of *a' la facon du pays*. Like fur-trade historians referred to in previous chapters, Kinsella reveals his bias in his representation of "Indian" women: he describes Linda as a "bad" squaw-like drudge who will be abandoned by Silas when he returns home to his "good" woman, Sadie One Wound, who deserves his love. He reveals his white-christian bias, also like fur trade historians, when he justifies Silas's decision to "give it a try" with Linda if the relationship with the "good" woman doesn't work out.[22] In other words, like some fur-trade historians who privilege white idealism, Kinsella covertly promotes the idea that a "good" woman back home is preferable to Linda Star, a "bad" street-woman.

Kinsella's story also promotes stereotypes and images that serve a white ideal in his construction of dialogue between Linda and Silas. For example, when she expresses her feelings to Silas, Linda says: "I is like for us to get married ... we could go away someplace where nobody knows us ... or we could go back to where you live ... I don't think I would mind live on a reserve if I with you ... I go anywhere you want me to."[23] The dialogue is problematic: whereas he represents Linda Star as assertively—perhaps even aggressively—articulating her intent, engaging in monetary exchanges, and exercising specific skills in order to never make "less than $100 a day," Kinsella characterizes Linda as communicating in a very child-like language.[24] I connect his representation of Linda's voice to monosyllabic "Indian" characters so popular in early films and television.

Kinsella's story further promotes stereotypes and images that serve a white ideal in his placement of Linda in relationships that are victimizing, abusive, and dehumanizing. First, he creates for Linda a history of victimization and abuse: she comes onto the page like a dehumanized squaw, physically and sexually abused by her reserve father. Second, already dehumanized, Linda takes up with another abuser, Clifton Black, whom she describes as "my old man."[25] According to Linda, they "don't live together or nothing but he looks out for [her] if a trick gives [her] trouble."[26] Third, she is revealed to be Kinsella's victimized, abused, and dehumanized squaw creation when she tells Silas that her pimp "take a real interest in me, you know what I mean. I give him some of my money and we get it on once in a while."[27] Fourth, Linda is revealed as reflecting the author's white ideals that spew out of the pimp Clifton's mouth. Clifton, the pimp, spews white supremacist notions of "Indian" women as white men's property or whores. And he dismisses Linda's dreams of settling down as unimportant because "all whores get ideas in their heads like that once in a while."[28] Kinsella's objectified stereotypical "Indian," Linda, appears to passively submit to the white pimp's cruel and dehumanizing treatment and to his physical, emotional, and psychological manipulation. The pimp uses her body for sexual gratification and economic exploitation; Clifton manipulates Linda's emotions to exploit her economically, and he tries to control her by creating a psychological dependence. Finally, Kinsella promotes the idea that Linda is an objectified stereotypical "Indian" who engages in casual sex with Silas, prematurely talks about moving in with him, and dreams of marriage and babies. Judged against the author's own white-christian-middle-class idealism, Linda appears immoral, a bad whore who deserves to be victimized, abused, and dehumanized.

Kinsella's story also promotes stereotypes and images that serve a white ideal in the characterization of Linda as an enslaved "Indian" whore owned and controlled by a white pimp. Clifton feels the need to flaunt his power over Linda when he notices her attraction to Silas. He seizes the opportunity to show Silas to whom Linda really belongs during a drug bust. When the police bust into Silas's room, the pimp hands Linda a package of drugs and tells her to stuff it: "Linda reach[es] down the front of her jeans and put[s] it between her legs."[29] Although the police pressure Linda to tell them where the drugs are and to whom they belong, she does not inform on him. At the police station, Clifton tells the police, "Hey, man. I can't let you bust my chick ... I'll take my own weight. The stuff's mine."[30] And, knowing full well that the drugs are not narcotics and that Linda will not be subject to a felony charge, the pimp orders her, "Give em the stuff, baby."[31] He later tells Silas, "I could have cleared the air right away but I seen the chance to show you who Linda really belongs to."[32] In his characterization of Linda, Kinsella covertly promotes the idea that she deserves to be enslaved, victimized, and abused. As author, he encourages readers to view Linda as a needy squaw-like whore who believes she deserves abuse. In fact, he scripts her saying to her new lover, "You have to kick my ass, Silas."[33]

Comparable to Kinsella's "Linda Star," Laurence's "The Loons" fosters cultural attitudes that condone simultaneously the violence and dehumanization of Indigenous-Metis girls/women in the author's representation of characters, place, and events. Laurence encourages negative cultural attitudes by selectively mirroring 20th-century Canada in her representation of two young girls, Piquette Tonnerre and Vanessa MacLeod. Piquette appears in story as mirroring 20th-century Canada's stereotypes of the suffering, helpless, and victimized offspring of "bad," rebellious "half-breeds," while Vanessa appears as mirroring the healthy, hopeful, and courageous descendants of "good" settlers.

Laurence further promotes negative cultural attitudes towards Indigenous-Metis women in her characterization of Piquette's and Vanessa's culture and language. The young "half-breed" girl appears in story without language or culture, speaking neither Cree nor French and belonging to neither the Galloping Mountain reservation Cree nor the Manawaka Scots-Irish and Ukrainians.[34] In contrast to Piquette's lack of culture and language, Vanessa figures into story enriched with language and culture, and she therefore functions as both the narrator and interpreter of events. As a narrator and interpreter who has never seen a "real Indian," Vanessa deems it necessary to romanticize Piquette as a kind of daughter of the forest/princess of nature, and a relation of Big Bear, Poundmaker, Tecumseh, and the Iroquois.[35] Even as an imagined relation of the so-called rebels Big Bear (Saulteaux) and Poundmaker (Cree), the warrior Tecumseh (Shawnee), and the savage "Iroquois who had eaten Father Brebeuf's heart," Piquette's presence in story stirs up settler anxiety and fosters cultural attitudes that justify uses of violence.[36]

In her representations of place/their respective homes, Laurence encourages cultural attitudes that legitimize violence against and dehumanization of Indigenous-Metis women. She describes, for example, Piquette's home as a squatter-like shack "made of poplar poles and chinked with mud" that was built by Jules Tonnerre, a wounded Metis rebel returning from Batoche after Riel was hung.[37] And, as her family home appears like an "Indian–half-breed" presence impeding colonial settlement, Laurence sets it against Vanessa's family and home to justify white-european-christian settlement. Thus, she represents the Tonnerre homeland as an increasingly growing and irritable threat "at the foot of the town hill" and their settlement as "a chaos of lean-tos, wooden packing cases, warped lumber, discarded car tires, ramshackle chicken coops, tangled strands of barbed wire and rusty tin cans."[38] Indeed, Piquette and her family are a continual reminder of "bad Indians/half-breeds" impeding the white-european-christian settlement of the prairies. Therefore, Vanessa—the embodiment of white-european-christian idealism—is used to narrate and interpret the story of the "bad Indians" not using the land productively. In representing Piquette as one of the "bad Indians" related to the so-called rebels Big Bear and Poundmaker, the warrior Tecumseh, and the savage Iroquois, Laurence stirs up cultural memories that justify the MacLeod family's cultural attitudes towards the Metis Tonnerre girl. Laurence's representation of Vanessa's home and homeland, on the other hand, legitimizes colonial presence, appearing as (from a previous story) a monumental brick house handed down through the generations as the "old Connor place."[39] That Laurence's representation of Vanessa's family home and homeland legitimizes colonization is most clear when she describes it as "some crusader's embattled fortress in a heathen wilderness, its rooms in a perpetual gloom."[40] When compared to Piquette's squatter-like shack and her people's encroaching presence, Vanessa's fortress-like home, the Connor homestead, and the colonial crusader connection justify white supremacist notions of manifest destiny—in other words, that Vanessa and her family have god-given rights to the land, while Piquette and her family do not.

Laurence encourages negative cultural attitudes towards Piquette by representing her as having a diseased, squaw-drudge–like body, a hopeless and abusive lifestyle, and a future without direction or dreams. Piquette's body and demeanour are thus described as a "lame leg held stiffly out, and her other foot scuffing the ground as she swung slowly back and forth"; the author also describes her straight, black, shoulder-length hair, and "broad coarse-featured face" that holds no expression.[41] Even her face seems to bear the remains of a hopeless and abusive lifestyle: Vanessa remembers Piquette's face as "blank, as though she no longer dwelt within her own skull, as though she had gone elsewhere."[42] In this passage, Vanessa— the symbolic representation of white-christian-middle-class values—sees Piquette only as an empty shell, a diseased squaw-drudge who repulses her. In fact, she concludes that even "as an Indian Piquette was a dead loss."[43] Soon Vanessa's fascination with Piquette wears off, and she whimsically dismisses from her life the young "half-breed" girl because "I could not reach Piquette at all, and I soon lost interest in trying."[44]

Laurence moves the plot forward by relying on stereotypes that discourage healthy representations of Indigenous women, and therefore promote negative cultural attitudes. She characterizes an older Piquette as a motherless, poor, suffering, and helpless victim of racism and sexism. Motherless, Piquette appears in story as the daughter of Lazarus Tonnerre and an unnamed mother who abandoned the family. In contrast to the unnamed and un-storied mother, her paternal relatives are described as Canadian Pacific Railway (CPR) men who worked as casual labourers and too often relied on relief payments. Impoverished, Piquette and her siblings are described as being "totally unfamiliar with laughter" when they "knock[ed] at the doors of the town's brick houses and offer[ed]" lard-pails of bruised wild strawberries for sale.[45] Suffering, Piquette is made to look after the family when "old Jules, or his son Lazarus, would get mixed up in a Saturday-night brawl ... howl drunkenly among the offended shoppers on Main Street," and consequently spend "the night in the barred cell underneath the Court House."[46] Victimized, Piquette embodies the squaw-like drudge who works without reward or compensation as housekeeper, cook, and laundress for her brothers and father.

Moving the plot forward, Laurence places her young "half-breed" character in the MacLeod family summer home, a white-christian-patriarchal-middle-class space dominated by negative stereotypes of Indigenous people that colour the reader's perceptions of Piquette. Dr. MacLeod, his wife, and his mother fill this white space with racist stereotypes that justify their treatment of and beliefs about "half-breed" people. First, Dr. MacLeod's wife and mother rely on racist stereotypes of dirty and unhealthy "half-breed Indians" to dissuade the doctor from inviting Piquette to stay with them for the summer. In fact, Mrs. MacLeod reveals her racist beliefs about "half-breed Indians" when she raises the argument that Piquette will infect their home and family with tuberculosis and lice. Her racist beliefs perpetuate stereotypes of diseased "half-breeds," and she therefore tries to convince the family that Piquette does not deserve basic human consideration. Second, Dr. MacLeod then reverts to stereotypical and patriarchal beliefs about Indigenous women as commodities (things that can be owned and manipulated) when he uses Piquette to broker a deal with his reluctant wife. He uses Piquette as leverage to convince his wife that she can "be company for Vanessa"[47] and deems Piquette, "nits or not," a useful companion for their daughter.[48]

As Laurence brings her story to a conclusion, both Vanessa and Piquette appear matured and grown up: Vanessa seems politically awakened, and Piquette seems unguarded and unmasked. In fact, Laurence characterizes Vanessa as seeing Piquette anew. To a seemingly politically awakened Vanessa, Piquette appears almost friendly. She realizes, "I really did see her, for the first and only time in all the years we had both lived in the same town. Her defiant face, momentarily, became unguarded and unmasked, and in her eyes there was a terrifying hope."[49] An unguarded and unmasked Piquette tells Vanessa about her upcoming marriage to "an English fella, [who] works in the stockyards in the city."[50] Vanessa realizes the "half-breed" girl has "been forced to seek the very things she so bitterly rejected."[51] In the end, however, Laurence characterizes Piquette in accordance with stereotypes that encourage negative cultural attitudes towards Indigenous women. For example, Piquette returns home to her father's squatter-like shack after a failed marriage to the (white) "English fella," without financial resources, without apparent job skills, and with dependants. Such representations encourage cultural beliefs that all Indigenous women are burdensome to hard-working (read as white) taxpayers, and therefore foster cultural attitudes that legitimize, as a final solution, extermination.

What's interesting is that, as the story draws to a close, Laurence does indeed kill off Piquette, a victim of her own vices.[52] While Laurence may have deliberately depicted Piquette as a victim of her own vices to effect "closure on the narrating of a Metis woman's life," like Maeser-Lemieux, "I am disappointed" but certainly not surprised by the tragic end to Piquette's life. Maeser-Lemieux offers an historical context for the failure of mixed cultural relations and the consequential death of Indigenous women.[53] When she connects Piquette to "the shadow side of the [princess] arche-type," represented in literature as savage and lustful, she encourages read-ers to see Laurence's representations of her as a shadowed, savage, and lustful squaw who is deservedly abandoned by her white husband.[54] To be written into the story as a "good Indian," squaw-like characters, such as Piquette, must be represented as defying their relations, exiling themselves from their community, and becoming white.[55] Unfortunately, as Maeser-Lemieux reminds us using Rayna Green's "The Pocahontas Perplex," characters such as Piquette must also "share in the same vices attributed to Indian men—drunkenness, stupidity, thievery—and they [must] live in shacks on the edge of town rather than in a woodland paradise."[56]

From my point of view, as a widely read Nehiowe-Metis-Anishinaabekwe reader and literary critic of Indigenous literatures, Margaret Laurence's depiction of Piquette Tonnerre, like William Patrick Kinsella's Linda Star, is very problematic because few readers understand the complex dynamics of racism and sexism, and particularly the way that patriar-chy operates in Indigenous women's lives. Characters such as Piquette and Linda Star are described, according to Maeser-Lemieux, "in degraded sensual imagery" to contrast the "good" woman of "patriarchy in whom lust and other vices are presumably absent."[57] As moral degradation, lust, and other vices are used to characterize representations of Indigenous women in literature, writers' decisions to kill them off appear justified. And, consequently, literary plots that kill off "Indian" women covertly promote cultural attitudes that foster dehumanization of and violence against Indigenous women.

Can readers of fiction discern differences between real Indigenous girls/ women and literary characters such as Laurence's "half-breed" Piquette Tonnerre and Kinsella's "Indian" Linda Star? Gordon Johnston claims most cannot. He explains that it is only exceptional student-readers who "see [characters like] Uncas and Magua in *The Last of the Mohicans* as anything but realistic and, hence, as inaccurate, racist distortions."[58] He argues that symbolic figures must be challenged and deconstructed because most readers believe them to be real. Johnston further cautions that "many writers of popular fictions ... either exploit or use uncritically ... racist images, and so, perpetuate the problem."[59] Comparably, the *Report of the Aboriginal Justice Inquiry of Manitoba* concluded, in Canada's shameful attitude towards Helen Betty Osborne's murder, that racist images and stereotypes encourage cultural attitudes that justify violence against Indigenous women. In fact, as I was writing the original manuscript for this book in late 1994, three Indigenous women's bodies (apparently buried for some time) were discovered just outside of Saskatoon. Since that gruesome discovery, the bodies were identified as being the remains of 30-year-old Eva Taysup, 16-year-old Shelley Napope, and 22-year-old Calinda Waterhen. Although convicted murderer John Crawford had already been imprisoned for manslaughter in Lethbridge, Alberta, for killing 35-year-old Mary Jane Serloin, he was released from jail and then brutally raped Janet Sylvester and Theresa Kematch in Saskatoon after he murdered Taysup, Napope, and Waterhen. And, as I do when I hear of any murder, I anticipated some kind of expression of concern (perhaps even outrage). I believe that the public saw Taysup, Napope, Waterhen, and Sylvestre only as stereotypical "Indian" women, and there was therefore little reaction to their brutal murders, whether from feminist groups, First Nations or Metis communities, the Federation of Saskatchewan Indian Nations, the Metis Nation of Saskatchewan, the government of Canada, the government of Saskatchewan, or members of the press. At that time, and for a long time afterwards, there were no feminist groups claiming Taysup, Napope, and Waterhen as "sisters" to be mourned. There were no communities acknowledging Taysup, Napope, and Waterhen as granddaughters, daughters, nieces, sisters, aunts, and mothers. There were no political organizations or governments deeming their lives important. Nor did the press respectfully eulogize their existence on this earth in comparable ways to their stories of white female murder victims. Granted, the Saskatoon *Star Phoenix*, the newspaper that, at that time, carried my bimonthly "Native Affairs" column, included interviews with family and friends of Shelley Napope, but few substantive media stories acknowledged their existence as human beings whose lives mattered. Instead of connecting their lives to dreams, aspirations, hopes, and loved ones, the newspaper stories that were eventually written described Taysup, Napope, and Waterhen as "part of the downtown bar scene" and women who "frequented downtown bars." Rather than representing them as individual human beings who were brutally murdered, the press conveniently grouped them in accordance with stereotypical representations. It frustrated me that depictions of Taysup, Napope, and Waterhen were drawn from the stereotypes of Indigenous women and the miserable conditions that imprisoned their lives. It seemed to me that such representations condoned the rape and killing of these women, as well as mainstream attitudes towards their murders. As it was so obvious that the mainstream apathy towards their murders was rooted in racism, sexism, and white-christian-patriarchal classism, I wondered how the public would react if the murder victims had been white. A telling example of white bias is represented in a *Star Phoenix* article from January 21, 1995, that discribed the serial killer as "a quiet man" who "lived with his mother ... [and] who has merely gone from being a suspect to a person accused of a horrific series of crimes."[60] As was revealed in the reporting of these gruesome murders, there is a clear connection between stereotypes, cultural attitudes, violence against, and murder of Indigenous women. And, as the numbers of missing and murdered Indigenous women in Canada continue to grow (to date, well over 1,000), I am absolutely convinced that most readers cannot distinguish real women from fictional characters. Moreover, how many white writers such as Kinsella and Laurence understand that even though many of us grew up in extreme poverty, with many social problems, and often only a little hope, we are not statistics? Or that we are human beings deserving of basic human rights and protection under the law? Few white writers before the emergence of contemporary bodies of Indigenous women's writing (generally) and the publication of Maria Campbell's *Halfbreed* (specifically) represented Indigenous women as cultured, strong, resourceful, self-determining, and self-governing female relations who offer healthy and wholesome examples for constituting Being.

These are the loves of my life: my grandchildren, Alijah-Blue, Lincoln, Alizeah, and Angelina.

CHAPTER FIVE

Maria Campbell's *Halfbreed*: A Politicized Text for Re-membering Being

indigenous writers, we gather on this meeting ground.
this burial ground that holds bones of thought. this living ground
that is ancient and sacred and new, like a song sung by each gen-
eration. like the landscape of grandmothers. like the spiritual
place that is inside each of us. where our ancestors' thoughts are
and writing roots us to this place, to the trees, to the land, to each
other. all connected.
　　—Kateri Akiwenzie-Damm, "this is where we stand our ground"

Maria Campbell's 1973 fictional autobiography *Halfbreed*[1] challenges existing stereotypes and images of Indigenous women by providing a vivid Spiritual, social, political, and economic context of her own "half-breed"–Cree way of life. Following in the literary trails set down by writers such as Pauline Johnson (1861–1913; Mohawk) and Mourning Dove (1888–1936; Okanagan), Campbell politicizes her writing to speak and write her way out of the assumptions that Indigenous women are "drenched in," to borrow from Adrienne Rich's discourse on the socialization of women in "When We Dead Awaken: Writing as Re-vision."[2] By politicizing her writing, she begins to understand how her "half-breed" identity has been constructed by white-eurocanadian-christian patriarchy. Through the act of writing, the author analyzes her own life and community, and then connects her "half-breed" people's spatial and Spiritual exile to the colonization of early Canada.[3] Inevitably, *Halfbreed* awakens Indigenous political consciousness to racism, sexism, and colonization. Indeed, Campbell's text is an important legacy for Indigenous women because it represents Cheechum, Grannie Campbell, Qua Chich, Grannie Dubuque, and her mother as signifying relations and survivors of the oppressive Canadian colonial regime, patriarchal dominance, and systemic racism and sexism.

Even now in 2015 in Canada—42 years after its original publication—*Halfbreed* is an important book that reveals Campbell's writing in English to be an inspiring political act that uses the fictional autobiographical story form to re-member herself to culturally significant female relations, thus encouraging possibilities for renewed cultural relations. For Campbell—a colonized and oppressed woman in Canada between 1940, the year of her birth, and 1973, the year of *Halfbreed*'s publication—writing became a political act that allowed her to re-member herself as a "half-breed"–Cree woman who occupies the textual space to challenge eurocanadian patriarchy, colonization, racism, and sexism. In the textual space that she occupies, Campbell names her oppressor; documents unjust systems, laws, and processes; and rejects culturally irrelevant christian beliefs and practices. A de-colonized, liberated, and re-membered "half-breed"–Cree woman, the author claims the textual space for the resettlement of all her relations. The former predominantly white textual space thus becomes enriched with both Indigenous–half-breed ideology and *wahkohtowin,* a kinship system that radiates from a Metis-Nehiowewin narrative memory.[4] By inspiriting her text with a culture-specific ideology and relational system, Campbell politicizes the deconstruction of easy squaw, Indian princess, and helpless victim stereotypes by re-membering herself to revolutionary, resourceful, dynamic, and adaptive women.

Wielding the barrel of a pen, Campbell politicizes writing to speak and write her way out of the assumptions Indigenous women are drenched in. Writing and then supporting the publishing of *Halfbreed* proved to be a courageously political act that documented and acknowledged one "half-breed"–Cree woman's life in racist and sexist 1970s Canada. Perhaps the strongest evidence that Campbell politicizes the act of writing when she takes up the barrel of the pen is her use of English, which she uses to indict sexism, racism, and colonization. When she places the words in text, "I write this for all of you, to tell you what it is like to be a Halfbreed woman in our country," Campbell talks back to those who dis-membered and colonized her Being.[5]

Talking back to oppressors and colonizers, she politicizes her writing by placing the word *"half-breed"* in text to name herself. Dr. Howard Adams (Metis) explains that while the term *"half-breed"* was used historically by european traders to identify someone as part "Indian" and part white, "halfbreed people did not have a choice as to whether they would be Indians or white or in-between; society defined them as members of the native society and it still does today."[6] As *"half-breed"* has "become a vulgar expression" today, the term *Metis* is used in its place as a polite term.[7] When placed in Campbell's occupied space, then, the word functions as a disturbing and shameful reminder of Canada's racist attitudes towards her people.

Campbell reveals the act of writing to be a political act when she dismantles constructs that imprison her identity, using her text instead to re-member herself to Cheechum, the niece of guerrilla warrior Gabriel Dumont. As such, Campbell uses the text to create connections between her own life and the warrior-like Cheechum, who tenaciously clung to her Cree-ness despite numerous and powerful threats from armed colonizers. She occupies the space to re-member herself in text to the courageous Cheechum who "hated to see the settlers come, and as they settled on what she believed was our land, she ignored them and refused to acknowledge them even when passing on the road."[8] Campbell occupies the space, as well, to re-member herself to women like her great-grandmother who rejected outright christianity: she recalls her Cheechum saying, "If there was such a thing as hell then she had lived there; nothing after death could be worse!"[9] Cheechum had lived through hell during her marriage to "Chee-pie-hoos/Evil-spirit-jumping-up-and-down," the author's great-grandfather from Edinburgh, Scotland, whom Campbell indicts as a sexist and an abuser of women. A merchant who ran the Hudson's Bay store, "Chee-pie-hoos" regarded Cheechum as an easy squaw, whom he believed "was having affairs with all the Halfbreeds in the area."[10] Although she married such an abuser, Cheechum defiantly resisted any kind of domination and chose instead to fight back during the Metis resistance in 1885. Cheechum gathered information, ammunition, and supplies to give to the resisters at Batoche, while Chee-pie-hoos collaborated with the North West Mounted Police. When the old man discovered Cheechum's support of the "half-breed fighters," he stripped her naked and beat her in public. Later, Chee-pie-hoos (Campbell's great-grandfather) mysteriously died, and Cheechum joined her Cree mother's people in lands now designated as Prince Albert National Park. As Campbell re-members herself to Cheechum's "Indian" relations, her text becomes an occupied space for the resettlement of her paternal ancestors, who "were never part of a reserve, as they weren't present when the treaty-makers came."[11]

And, as the author places Cheechum's stories in text, she re-members herself to a courageous, self-sufficient Cree woman who hunted, trapped, gathered food, built her house, raised her family, and rejected welfare and old-age pension. When Campbell recalls the old woman's armed stand-off with the RCMP, she creates a space for legitimate "Indian" dissent by politicizing the old woman's response to armed colonizers: Cheechum locked her door, loaded her rifle, and fired shots over the heads of armed white men.[12] When she relates herself in text to Cheechum, Campbell connects her life to a history of resistance in her family. As an Indigenous woman, Cheechum refused to be dis-membered from knowledge, values, and beliefs derived from closeness to the land. Having lived through many kinds of changes, Cheechum resisted mainstream influences and spoke openly about the politics of war, the church, the roles of men and women, and the government. After Campbell's mother died, Cheechum, who never found comfort in church or prayer, provided her granddaughter with strength and support. As Cheechum viewed long hours of prayer as "a pure waste of time" and the concept of heaven or hell futile, the old woman taught her granddaughter instead to see beauty in all living things. She taught Campbell "that inside each thing a Spirit lived, that it was vital too, regardless of whether it was only a leaf or a blade of grass, and [that] by recognizing its life and beauty" she was acknowledging god.[13] In this passage, Campbell politicizes the act of writing to re-member herself to

Cheechum, a deeply Spiritual woman who resisted white-euorcanadian-christian patriarchy's authority.

The author dismantles constructs of Indigenous women, politicizes the act of writing, and occupies the textual space to re-member herself, as well, to Grandma Campbell, a "Vandal" woman whose family had been involved in the 1885 Resistance. The wife of Cheechum's son, Grandma Campbell is represented as a fiercely determined woman who, after her husband's death, "went to a white community ... to cut brush for seventy-five cents an acre."[14] Re-membered in text to the author's cultural body, Grandma Campbell defies stereotypes as she is represented as a legendarily strong, resourceful, and self-sufficient woman. Campbell writes, "Because they [Grannie Campbell and her children] had only one team of horses and Dad used these to work for other people, Grannie on many occasions pulled the plough herself."[15] Totally self-sufficient, like Cheechum, Grannie Campbell became angry when her son (Campbell's father) announced that he would take care of her, and she reminded him that "he had a family to worry about and what she did was none of his business."[16] Until she was quite old, "she brushed and cleared the settlers' land, picked their stones, delivered their babies, and looked after them when they were sick."[17] By relating herself in text to both Grannie Campbell and Cheechum, Campbell politicizes the act of writing to reattach her Being to a maternal lineage that throughout history resisted white-eurocanadian patriarchy's oppression.

Campbell further uses writing in English as a political act when she re-members herself to Qua Chich, a self-determining and self-governing woman whose representation defies stereotypes of suffering, victimized Indigenous women. Campbell places Qua Chich in the textual space as a survivor of the government's treaty-making interventions, her relocation to an Indian reserve, her marriage to a man who leaves her a widow, and the destitution and poverty that afflicted her sisters and brothers. She defies stereotypes of suffering, victimized Indigenous women, as Campbell represents her as a strange old lady who rarely lent out money and cussed at her dog in Cree. Her aunt Qua Chich was considered quite wealthy because she "owned many cows and horses as well as a big two-storey house" and maintained her home and property long after her husband's death.[18] While Campbell's descriptions of the old lady as stingy with money and reluctant to lend money without a formal contract seem to be unflattering and hardly like the compassionate Grannie Campbell and Cheechum, Qua Chich's business skills, along with her courage and determination, further exemplify the strong and resourceful female relations that enrich the author's text.[19]

When Campbell places her maternal relations in text alongside the self-governing Qua Chich, the fiercely determined Grannie Campbell, and the warrior-like Cheechum, she represents Mother and Grannie Dubuque as convent-educated treaty "Indian" women who defy stereotypical images. In her descriptions of her mother and maternal grandmother, however, the author performs a political act when she uses writing to connect her maternal relations to a painful history of christian oppression. As she connects the mother and grandmother to the convent and patriarchy, Campbell begins to understand how christianity is a powerful force of colonization that severely eroded possibilities for Cree Spiritual transmission. Campbell recalls that even when the christians' ungodly ways were so obviously apparent, her mother rarely spoke out against the church or the priests. In fact, she describes her mother as quietly submissive, with an undaunting and unquestioning faith in the christian god, even when the fat priest selfishly ate what little food they had. Her mother, she writes, "accepted it all as she did so many things because it was sacred and of God."[20] The priest, by comparison, showed no respect for what was sacred to them, for he stole from the "Indian's Sundance Pole ... [things] that belonged to the Great Spirit."[21] Despite her seemingly blind faith in christianity, the mother appears in Campbell's occupied textual space as a culturally significant female relation who, as a lover of books and music, defies stereotypical images of voiceless, dumb, and uncultured squaws. Neither an Indian princess nor a squaw drudge, the mother is re-membered in text as a hard-working and respectful woman who "loved books and music and spent many hours reading."[22]

In her representation of Grannie Dubuque, Campbell uses writing as a political act to talk back to the colonizer about christian indoctrination, arranged marriages, and white idealism. Grannie Dubuque is re-membered into Campbell's text as a female child raised in a christian convent. Barely a teenager, Granny Dubuque is forced into an arranged marriage with a Frenchman, Pierre Dubuque. Although her relationship with the Frenchman is short-lived—because he dies from an illness very early in their marriage—Grannie Dubuque appears to have accumulated a wealth of knowledge. Thus, when she visits Maria and her siblings, Grannie Dubuque lights up their impoverished home with imagination and laughter. During visits, she encourages Maria and her siblings to imagine their basic diet (meat, potatoes, bannock, lard and tea) as fancy salads and chicken à la king on a fancy tablecloth.[23] Thus, while she seems to be privileging a white idealism, symbolized as imagined fancy foods, Grannie Dubuque defies stereotypical representations as an imaginative and resourceful woman who liberates Maria and her siblings from colonial oppression.

In later years, looking back more wisely upon her maternal family's relationship to christianity, the author connects christianity to a powerful ideological force that justifies colonization. When Campbell describes christian priests as men "coming in front of the colonizer,"[24] she uses her text to hold "the priest [who] had total power in the community" accountable for colonization.[25] Thus, she politicizes the act of writing to speak out against the forces of christianity that "are now incorporating Indigenous ceremonies and rituals."[26] Synthesizing Indigenous Spirituality and christianity is much more dangerous, she says, because then "the priest ends up becoming the shaman in the community."[27] While her tone may seem bitter to some, Campbell politicizes her writing to make clear that, when she was a young girl, her dreams, hopes, and ambitions were shattered by christian patriarchal intrusions, extreme poverty, racism, and sexism.

Campbell was 33 years old when she politicized the act of writing to reexamine old truths associated with colonialism. Although her political consciousness of racism, sexism, and colonization grows from an emotional place, Campbell's anger and frustration does not consume her. Instead of giving in to her emotions, returning to prostitution and drugs, she performs a political act in writing about her oppression.[28] For Campbell, writing becomes a political act of resistance that allows her to envision renewed relations with her family and community. With a renewed vision, Campbell uses written English to historicize colonial oppression, racism, and sexism, and it becomes a story that has rarely been told by Indigenous women in North America. A survivor, she refuses to let her ancestors' sufferings be whitewashed by liberal do-gooders "killing us with their liberal gentleness."[29] Liberalism, Campbell claims, encourages Canadians to believe that horrible racism doesn't exist in this country. In her indictment of colonization, she draws comparisons to the atrocities committed by the Nazis in the 1940s in Germany: "Nobody ever would believe that in Saskatchewan at the same time people were loaded into cattle cars, not having bathrooms or facilities, and were carted off, hauled some place, and dumped off in the middle of the snow—and some of those people dying."[30] Here Campbell encourages other Indigenous writers to hold Canada accountable for its oppression of Metis people. As she calls out to other Indigenous writers to "tell those stories ourselves," she occupies the textual space in order to illuminate internalized colonization.[31]

Internalized colonialism, Cheechum taught her, is reflected in colonized people's self-hate and their idealization of white culture. It was apparent in the "half-breeds" who came west, leaving good homes behind them. While their westward journey was marked by overwhelming struggles, according to Cheechum, they persevered because they relied on cultural knowledge and community support. Eventually, however, white idealism undermined their collective dreams, and they began to fight and hate each other. Cheechum's words, and Campbell's memory of them, are important because they relate to internalized colonialism as it is manifested in an overpowering desire for white materialism. Internalized colonialism is also connected to memories of her father: his failed dreams, reliance on alcohol, and physical abuse of Cheechum and her mother. She remembers that her father's dreams died after failed attempts to politicize the community. Feeling rejected by his own people, he turned to alcohol and began abusing the womenfolk. In writing about her father's alcoholism and domestic violence, Campbell connects his failures to the Metis people's unrealized dreams and hopes, internalized colonization, and spatial exile.[32]

The author uses writing to politicize her own internalized colonialism, as she remembers privileging white idealism. She includes in her story memories of the "Germans" and "Swedes," who seemed to her the wealthiest and most beautiful people because they had "pretty cloth for dresses," were able to afford apples and oranges, and had "toothbrushes

Maria Campbell's *Halfbreed* | 79

and brushed their teeth every day."[33] This dream, which represents an idealization of white culture, blinds Campbell to the dangers of life with the abuser and addict whom she marries. In her memories of her relationship to the abuser and addict, Campbell reveals white idealism to be a powerful force. Indeed, even when her white husband beats, belittles, and eventually deserts her, Campbell stays with him.[34] Although it is a powerful force connected to internalized colonialism, white idealism does not mute the stories or undermine the memories of Campbell's strong, vital, and resourceful female relations. In fact, she uses writing as a political tool to re-member herself to powerful relations, like Cheechum, whose memories help her to overcome internalized colonialism and white idealism.

A politicized Indigenous writer, Campbell encouraged many Indigenous people to begin writing, and her text initiated the process of representing Indigenous women both positively and knowledgeably. In *Contemporary Challenges: Conversations with Canadian Native Authors*, Hartmut Lutz respectfully acknowledges *Halfbreed* as a bestseller and the most important book authored by a Native Canadian.[35] Lenore Keeshig-Tobias (using Daniel David Moses's words) describes Campbell as the mother of contemporary Indigenous literatures and writers.[36] Indeed, Jeannette Armstrong describes *Halfbreed* as "an important book in terms of Native literature."[37] Beth Cuthand insists that "*Halfbreed* is a classic. If people are studying Canadian Native literature, they have to read it."[38] Jordan Wheeler claims that *Halfbreed* "still has a record as the bestselling first book by anybody in Canadian history."[39] Emma LaRocque describes *Halfbreed* as a "powerful mirror to Canadian society."[40] As the next chapter illustrates, Campbell's *Halfbreed* also inspired me to use writing as a political act: in my criticism and scholarship I, too, occupy written English to re-settle Kah' Ki Yaw Niwakomanak and renew Manitoukwe cultural relations.

CHAPTER SIX

Re-calling Signifying Female Relations to Transform Being

*indigenous writers. this is the ground upon which we stand. we
know this ground and this ground knows us. she recognizes our
ancestors in us. she knows our genealogy. we carry this knowing
and so we will not be moved. we will not be muted. even if our
stories are ignored. our tongues ripped from our throats. our poetry ridiculed. our mouths slapped. we will not be moved. no matter how many times the maps are changed. the borders shifted.
the lines drawn. we will not be moved.
indigenous writers. this is the ground upon which we stand. this
is the motherland. the gathering place. the place for remember-
ing, for singing, for telling stories, for honouring the bones of our
ancestors. this is why we stand firm. why we will not be moved.*

—Kateri Akiwenzie-Damm, "this is where we stand our ground"

When I come to writing, I carry with me an ancient lineage of
mothers and grandmothers that roots me to the Earth. Thus,
when I come to the page, "this meeting ground," like Campbell and
Iskwewak Kah' Ki Yaw Ni Wahkomakanak who came before me, I use
writing as a political act to claim the written in English textual space
for the re-settlement of signifying Manitoukwe relations and Iskwewak
Kah' Ki Yaw Ni Wahkomakanak in stories and books. For as Kateri
Akiwenzie-Damm writes, "this is our territory, this is indigenous

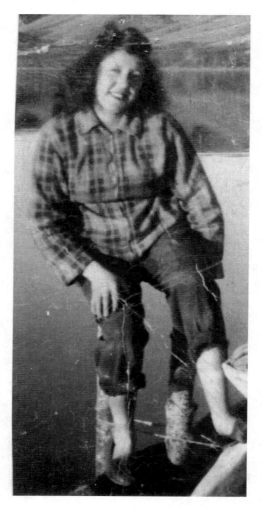

My mother, Harriet Acoose, around 17 years
old at Marival, Saskatchewan.

land."[1] I come to the page, "this gathering of nations," a cultured Nehiowe-
Metis-Anishinaabekwe who reasons critically from within a culture-specific
relational system of signification.[2] And, I control the English language in
my usage of it. For example, when I use the word *cultured*, I call attention
to the way my Being as a contemporary Nehiowe-Metis-Anishinaabekwe
requires continuous learning, studying, and growing with ancestral teachings. And when I use the word *Spirit*, I capitalize the *s* to illustrate my values.
As a contemporary Nehiowe-Metis-Anishinaabekwe, I realize and constitute

My maternal grandmother, Philomene Beaudin, in front of her house at the Marival Half-Breed Colony.

My maternal great-grandmother, Down Koochum: here she sits near her log cabin home at the Marival Half-Breed Colony.

My paternal Koochum, Madeline (O'Soup) Acoose.

meaning by attending to Spiritual teachings, honouring ancestors, nurturing all the relations, relearning my languages, participating in ceremonies, and contributing to the making of knowledge, government, art, music, and dance. As I enter critical and storied territories to make meaning, I carry with me my Nehiowe-Metis-Anishinaabe cultures and relational systems. Thus, my making of knowledge does not grow *in relation to* the English language, but rather *in relations with* it. In other words, I do not look at the English language as an all-knowing, all-being referent or source of meaning. I use it along with my own systems of knowledge to produce/create meaning.

I employ this critical strategy to moderate the eurocentric authority of English because, like my ancestors who in 1876 signed Treaty 4, I envision negotiating space for Being Nehiowe-Metis-Anishinaabekwe in both the textual and physical space in Canada. While writing my doctoral dissertation (from which some of these ideas grew), the birth of my first granddaughter and the making of the film *Finding Dawn*[3] profoundly unsettled my Being. I place my memories of those life-changing and Spiritually unsettling experiences here to offer them back to this textual "motherland."

My first granddaughter Angelina-Ogimaakwe's birth is very important because she was at birth the only future link for my maternal lineage. The daughter of my son Blue and his then-partner Nicole Figueroa, my precious Angelina-Ogimaakwe, came into the world three months premature, just a little under two pounds. While the doctors advised us to enjoy every second we had with her, they also told us not to touch her. We spent our moments looking upon her fragile little body as machines kept her alive. Because I was terrified and uncertain how to support Blue and Nicole, I told them stories about my paternal legendary Acoose ancestors. Also, against the doctor's advice, I told my son Blue to touch his daughter, to pass on the strength of Spiritual ancestors. He told me then that he was under a lot of pressure and didn't need "my bullshit," since the doctors and the neonatal machines were keeping her alive. I was deeply hurt by the disrespectful way he spoke to me and what I perceived to be his callous disregard for the few teachings I offered. Eventually, I went home and cried long into the night, all the while feeling that I should be at the hospital beside my granddaughter, daughter-in-law, and son.

The next morning I retreated to my home office, and I cried some more because I felt like I was mourning the loss of ancient ancestral ways. In my office that morning, I could only think about strategies for living one moment to the next. Then, I noticed a book still encased in plastic wrap on my desk. Without much thought, I picked it up, because stories always comforted me. The book immediately fell open to a poem by Jace Weaver called "Blue."[4] Since my second son, Angelina's father, is named Blue, I turned to the poem hoping to find some comfort, some way to help me understand how to move through the days ahead.

Reading the poem and eventually sharing it with Blue transformed our troubled and troubling relations. Weaver's poem, which appears in *Other Words: American Indian Literature, Law, and Culture*, begins with the lines

> The sun crowns the horizon mountains
> Like a child being pushed from its mother's womb.
> Born out of the earth this day as any other,
> A ceaseless cycle of birth, death, and rebirth.[5]

As a Nehiowe-Metis-Anishinaabekwe, I interpreted these lines as confirming my own Spiritual beliefs about Manitoukwe. The words "mother's womb," as well as "cycle of birth, death, and rebirth," ignited Spiritual memories of that ancient lineage of grandmothers. The words "born out of the earth" re-membered me to Iskwewak Kah' Ki Yaw Ni Wahkomakanak, all the relations that gave me life. Indeed, I interpreted Weaver's joining of the words "born out of the earth" to "this day as any other" as a legitimization and recognition of the ongoing relevance of such Spiritual teachings.

Reading the poem and eventually sharing it with Blue encouraged me to draw on my own teachings of ancestors. I interpreted "The creatures of the night / Have packed away their voices. / And those of the day have yet to find their throats" as allusions to an ongoing ancestral system that relates all Beings philosophically and Spiritually. And, I related "creatures of the night" packing away their voices to ancestral memories that live in me. I also understood "those of the day have yet to find their throats" to mean young people like my son, who need to open themselves up to Spiritual ancestors. Reading the remainder of Weaver's poem, I realized how insignificant mere human relations are in the light of all Creation. I thought about the poet attempting to fix Being in both language and time when he writes, "It is the time the French call 'l'heure bleue', / The blue hour. / But it is not an hour but a moment, an instant, / Suspended between night and dawn." Like the poet, I felt that trying to fix Being can become futile, as an hour disappears into a moment, and then is suspended between night and day. Like the poet, I thought of that pre-dawn morning as the "blue hour," a time of ancestral presence when we're reminded to greet "the new day."

Reading Weaver's poem the morning after Angelina-Ogimaakwe's birth helped me to understand the strength of Spiritual teachings carried through stories. Reading "Blue" re-membered me to my human relations during a time of crisis, fear, and uncertainty. Because the poem is called "Blue," recalls cycles of birth and rebirth, relates Being to ancestors, and acknowledges the small voice of Elijah's god, I connected to it personally. My youngest son's name is Blue; my granddaughter Angelina had just been born; my son had dismissed teachings about ancestral Spirit as unimportant; and Blue's first child's name is Alijah (a variation of Elijah). After I read the poem to Blue, he seemed to understand how a connection to Nehiowe-Metis-Anishinaabe ancestors might inspirit and anchor Angelina's Being.

In the days that followed, I demonstrated for him a ceremonial way of infusing Angelina's Being with the strength of ancestors. Each day, I sat beside the plastic cubicle that held my grandbaby's precious little body. And as Miswonigeesikokwe, placing my hand on the cubicle that held her precious little body, I called on Great-Spirited female ancestors to re-member her Being. Over and over again, I spoke the names of signifying female relations:

Harriet Acoose, my mother
Philomene Marie Beaudin-Desjarlais, my maternal grandmother
Therese Philomene Desjarlais, my Down Koochum/maternal great-grandmother
Pittwawekanepit, my maternal great-great-grandmother
Madeline O'Soup Acoose, my paternal Koochum

To their names, I added the names of my paternal male Acoose relations:

Fred Acoose, my father
Paul Acoose, paternal Mooshum
Samuel Acoose, my paternal great-grandfather
Qu'wich, my paternal great-great-grandfather

Ceremoniously as Miswonigeesikokwe, I called the Spirits of ancestors to re-member Angelina's Being. Ceremoniously, I named her spirit Ogimaakwe to re-member her Being to Iskwewak Kah' Ki Yaw Ni' Wahkomakanak and then all my Anishinaabe paternal relations. Looking back, I am grateful that I can re-member my Being to such powerful Spiritual relations, many of whom I lived with as a child. Without my connections to those once-living relations and the others I make through stories, I could not have called on ancestral Spirits to root my precious granddaughter's Being. Thus, when I write like all the Great-Spirited Indigenous female Creators who came before me, I occupy written English in books to renew and re-settle Iskwewak Kah' Ki Yaw Ni Wahkomakanak.

My granddaughter Angelina-Ogimaakwe's birth coincided with the time I spent with filmmaker Christine Welsh on *Finding Dawn*, a film about missing and murdered Indigenous women in Canada. It remains, for me, one of the most Spiritually unsettling projects I've worked on to date. So, on this page—here in the last chapter—I respectfully place in this "burial ground that holds bones of thought" the knowing, hearing, seeing, and feeling memories of the missing and murdered Indigenous women in Canada whose Spirits were unsettled in the making of the film.[6] On this page, "this landscape of grandmothers," I place my memories of their lives, my memories of their voices, my memories of their pain, and my memories of their stories.[7] Here, I place my memories in this "motherland" that re-members me to ancestors who speak through me, whose voices are re-membered to other voices, calling, "singing and laughing, and crying / telling stories, speaking poetry, asserting themselves. / calling out and answering. calling and listening and answering."[8] On this page, this "motherland," I re-member to an ancient lineage of mothers, of grand-mothers, and great-grandmothers my memories of the lives, voices, pain, and stories of all the missing and murdered Indigenous women.[9] Here on this page, I connect my memories of the stories of missing and murdered women in Canada to the birth of my first granddaughter, Angelina, who, as the culturally signifying Ogimaakwe, connects all my future relations to an ancient lineage of grandmothers, all the way back to the first Great-Spirited Creator-Mother.

Questions to Promote Critical Conversations

1. What do the epigraphs placed at the beginnings of each chapter contribute to the book?
2. What do Acoose's personal stories contribute to your understanding of violence against Indigenous women?
3. What do the names "Last Standing Women" or "Red Sky Woman" symbolize? What strategies would you use to formulate a response to this question?
4. The author repeatedly refers to "Great-Spirited" signifying relations. Why does she employ repetition in her usage of the terms? What do you think she means? What are the implications of her usage?
5. In regard to the missing and murdered Indigenous women in Canada, has reading *Iskwewak* encouraged you to "move beyond words," as Acoose claims we must?
6. Do you remember any of the names of the murdered Indigenous women acknowledged by Acoose? What do you think it implies when people remember the perpetrator's name rather than those of the victims?
7. Consider the word *re-member*, used throughout to convey a reattachment of signifying relations to Indigenous cultural bodies. Does this have personal significance for you?
8. Consider Acoose's use of post-apocalyptic stress syndrome (PASS). Discuss the intergenerational effects of PASS and post-traumatic stress disorder (PTSD).
9. Think about your own reading of early Canadian literature. Do you agree or disagree with Acoose's claims that the literature relies on stereotypes of Indigenous women? If you agree, identify and talk about some of the books, including the Indigenous female characters, and the cultural attitudes about them. If you disagree, explain why.

10. Discuss Acoose's claims that stereotypes foster cultural attitudes that justify violence against/murder of Indigenous women.
11. Is there some action you might take to contribute to the elimination of violence against Indigenous women?
12. Can you think about and put into action some strategies for community responses to violence against Indigenous women?
13. Has racism, sexism, or colonization affected your life?
14. Is violence against Indigenous women peculiar to Canada?
15. Acoose cites Campbell's *Halfbreed* as an important book for re-readings of Indigenous women's lives. Can you think of any other books you have read that encouraged you to re-examine old truths about Indigenous women?
16. Consider the word *violence*. Does the word mean physical harm to one's body? Are there other forms of violence perpetuated against women?

Notes

Chapter One: Iskwewak Kah' Ki Yaw Ni Wahkomakanak: Re-membering Being to Signifying Female Relations

1. Laurie Barron, "The CCF and the Development of Metis Colonies in Southern Saskatchewan During the Premiership of T.C. Douglas, 1944–1961," *The Canadian Journal of Native Studies* 10, no. 2 (1990): 243–70.
2. Emma LaRocque, interview in *Contemporary Challenges: Conversations with Contemporary Canadian Native Writers* (Saskatoon: Fifth House Publishers, 1991), 202.
3. Lawrence Gross, "*Bimaadiziwin*, or the 'Good Life,' as a Unifying Concept of Anishinaabe Religion," *American Indian Culture and Research Journal* 26, no. 1 (2002), 23.
4. LaRocque, *Contemporary Challenges*, 181.
5. Ibid.
6. Craig Womack, Daniel Heath Justice, and Chris Tueton, eds., *Reasoning Together: The Native Critics Collection* (Norman: University of Oklahoma Press, 2008), 404.

Chapter Two: Literature, Stereotypes, and Cultural Attitudes

1. Ngugi Wa Thiong'o, *Writers in Politics* (London: Heinemann Educational Books, 1981), 20.
2. Ibid.
3. Robert Berkhofer, *The Whiteman's Indian: Images of the American Indian from Columbus to the Present* (New York: Vintage Books, 1979), 4.
4. Ibid., 7.
5. Ibid., 9.
6. Raymond William Stedman, *Shadow of the Indians: Stereotypes in American Culture* (London: University of Oklahoma Press, 1989), 32.
7. Angelika Maeser-Lemieux, "The Metis in the Fiction of Margaret Laurence: From Outcast to Consort," in *The Native in Literature: Canadian and*

Comparative Perspectives, eds. Thomas King, Cheryl Calver, and Helen Hoy (Toronto: ECW Press, 1987), 125.

8. Stedman, *Shadow of the Indians,* 32.

9. Angelika Maeser-Lemieux, "The Metis in the Fiction of Margaret Laurence," 125.

10. Peter C. Newman, *Company of Adventurers* (Toronto: Penguin Books Canada, 1985), 271.

11. Ibid.

12. Kim Anderson, A *Recognition of Being: Reconstructing Native Womanhood* (Toronto: Sumach Press, 2000).

13. Ibid., 57–98.

14. Ibid., 58–59.

15. Howard Adams, *Prison of Grass: Canada From a Native Point of View* (Saskatoon: Fifth House Publishers, 1975).

16. Emma LaRocque, *Defeathering the Indian* (Agincourt, ON: Book Society of Canada, 1975).

17. Adams, *Prison of Grass,* 35–37.

18. Ibid, 38–39.

19. Ibid.

20. Beatrice Culleton, *In Search of April Raintree* (Winnipeg: Pemmican Publications, 1983), 66.

21. Margaret Anderson, "Sexism and the Social Construction of Knowledge," in *Thinking about Women: Sociological Perspectives on Sex and Gender* (New York: MacMillan, 1998), 29.

22. Ibid.

23. Thiong'o, *Writers in Politics,* 7.

24. Ibid., 15.

25. Ibid., 36.

26. Adams, *Prison of Grass,* 14.

27. Ibid.

28. Ibid.

29. Joan Rockwell, "A Theory of Literature in Society: The Hermeneutic Approach," *Sociological Review Monograph* 25 (1977): 32–42.

30. Paula Gunn Allen, *The Sacred Hoop: Recovering the Feminine in American Indian Traditions* (Boston: Beacon Press, 1986); Paula Gunn Allen, ed., *Spider Woman's Granddaughters: Traditional Tales and Contemporary Writing by Native American Women* (New York: Ballantine Books, 1989); Paula

Gunn Allen, *Grandmothers of the Light: A Medicine Woman's Sourcebook* (Boston: Beacon Press, 1991).

31. Marla Powers, "Sex Roles and Social Structures," in *Oglala Women: Myth, Ritual, and Reality* (Chicago: University of Chicago Press, 1983), 203.

32. Beatrice Medicine, "Warrior Woman—Sex Role Alternatives for Plains Indian Women," in *The Hidden Half: Studies of Plains Indian Women* (Lanham, MD: University Press of America, 1983), 267.

33. Lorraine Littlefield, "Women Traders in the Maritime Fur Trade," in *Native People, Native Lands: Canadian Indians, Inuit and Metis*, ed. Bruce Alden Cox (Ottawa: Carleton University Press, 1987), 173.

34. Priscilla Buffalohead, "Farmers Warriors Traders: A Fresh Look at Ojibway Women," *Minnesota History* 48 (1983): 236–44.

Chapter Three: Keeping the Fire: Iskwewak Kah' Ki Yaw Ni Wahkomakanak

1. Frantz Fanon, *The Wretched of the Earth* (New York: Grove Press, 1963).

2. Ibid., 11.

3. Ibid.

4. R. G. Thwaites, ed., *Jesuit Relations and Allied Documents*. 73 vols. (New York: Pageant Books, 1959).

5. Eleanor Leacock, "Montagnais Women and the Jesuit Program for Colonization," in *Myths of Male Dominance: Collected Articles on Women Cross-Culturally* (New York: Monthly Review Press, 1981), 45.

6. Ibid.

7. Ibid.

8. Priscilla Buffalohead, "Farmers Warriors Traders: A Fresh Look at Ojibway Women," *Minnesota History* 48 (1983): 236–44.

9. Patricia Albers, "New Perspectives on Plains Indian Women," in *The Hidden Half: Studies of Plains Indian Women* (Lanham, MD: University Press of America, 1983), 8.

10. Osennontion and Skonaganleh:ra, "Our World: According to Osennontion and Skonaganleh:ra," in *Canadian Woman Studies/les cahiers de la femme* (Toronto: York University, 1989), 7–19.

11. Albers, *The Hidden Half*, 1.

12. Jeanette Armstrong, "The Disempowerment of First North American Native Peoples and Empowerment Through Their Writing," in *An*

Anthology of Native Canadian Literature in English, eds. Daniel David Moses and Terry Goldie (Toronto: Oxford University Press, 1998), 242–45.

13. Emma LaRocque, preface to *Writing the Circle: Native Women of Western Canada*, eds. Jeanne Perreault and Sylvia Vance (Edmonton: NeWest Publishers, 1990), xx.

14. Tomson Highway, *Dry Lips Oughta Move to Kapuskasing* (Saskatoon: Fifth House Publishing, 1990).

15. Richard Wagamese, *Indian Horse* (Vancouver: Douglas and McIntyre, 2012).

16. Ibid., 55.

17. Ibid.

18. Ibid.

19. Ibid., 65.

20. Thomas King, *All My Relations: An Anthology of Contemporary Canadian Fiction* (Toronto: McClelland and Stewart, 1990), xi.

21. Independent Commission on International Humanitarian Issues, *Indigenous Peoples: A Global Quest for Justice* (London: Zed Books, 1987).

22. UN General Assembly, *United Nations Declaration on the Rights of Indigenous Peoples*: resolution/adopted by the General Assembly, October 2, 2007, A/RES/61/295.

23. Elder Dan Musqua, personal communication, December 2, 2009.

24. bell hooks, *Talking Back: Thinking Feminist, Thinking Black* (Toronto: Between the Lines, 1988), 6.

25. LaRocque, *Writing the Circle*, xviii.

26. Howard Adams, *Prison of Grass: Canada from a Native Point of View* (Saskatoon: Fifth House Publishers, 1975), 141.

27. LaRocque, *Writing the Circle*, xvii.

28. Maria Campbell, *Halfbreed* (Toronto: McClelland and Stewart, 1973).

29. LaRocque, *Writing the Circle*, xviii.

30. Adrianne Rich, "When We Dead Awaken: Writing as Re-Vision," in *On Secrets, Lies and Silence: Selected Prose 1966–1978* (New York: W.W. Norton, 1979), 33–49.

31. Connie Fife, ed., *The Colour of Resistance: A Contemporary Collection of Writing by Aboriginal Women* (Toronto: Sister Vision Press, 1993), 2.

32. Marilyn Dumont, *A Really Good Brown Girl* (London, ON: Brick Books, 1996); Joy Harjo and Gloria Bird, eds., *Reinventing the Enemy's Language: Contemporary Native Women's Writings of North America* (New York: Norton & Company, 1977); Lee Maracle, *Bobby Lee: Indian Rebel* (Toronto: Women's

Press, 1990), *I Am Woman* (North Vancouver: Write-on Press Publishers, 1988), and *Sojourner's Truth and Other Stories* (Vancouver: Press Gang Publishers, 1990); Marie Annharte Baker, *Being on the Moon* (Winlaw, British Columbia: Polestar Press, 1990); Jeannette Armstrong, *Slash* (Penticton: Theytus Books, 1988); Louise Erdrich, *Love Medicine* (Toronto: Bantam Books, 1984), *The Beet Queen* (Toronto: Bantam Books, 1986), and *Tracks* (New York: Harper & Row, 1988); Mary Crow Dog and Richard Erdoes, *Lakota Woman* (New York: HarperCollins, 1990); Agnes Grant, ed., *Our Bit of Truth: An Anthology of Canadian Native Literature* (Winnipeg: Pemmican Publications, 1990); Jeanne Perreault and Sylvia Vance, eds., *Writing the Circle: Native Women of Western Canada* (Edmonton: NeWest Publishers, 1990); Louise Halfe, *Bear Bones and Feathers* (Regina: Coteau Books, 1994); Beth Cuthand, *Voices in the Waterfall* (Vancouver: Lazara Press, 1989); Connie Fife, ed., *The Colour of Resistance: A Contemporary Collection of Writing by Aboriginal Women* (Toronto: Sister Vision Press, 1993).

33. Paula Gunn Allen, *The Sacred Hoop: Recovering the Feminine in American Indian Traditions* (Boston: Beacon Press, 1986), 3.

34. Alanis Obomsawin, *Kanehsatake: 270 Years of Resistance* (Toronto: National Film Board of Canada, 1993), 119 min.

35. "Court Adds to Membership Case Law," *Sage: Aboriginal News Publication* 4, no. 2 (1999).

36. Christine Welsh, *Finding Dawn* (Vancouver: National Film Board of Canada, 2006), 73 min.

Chapter Four: Stereotypes and Dis-membered Relations

1. *Report of the Aboriginal Justice Inquiry of Manitoba*, November 1999. http://www.ajic.mb.ca/volumeII/chapter1.html

2. Ibid., 11.

3. Ibid., 3.

4. Emma LaRocque, "Tides, Towns and Trains," in *Living the Changes*, ed. Joan Turner (Winnipeg: University of Manitoba Press, 1990), 87.

5. Ibid.

6. Marlene Nourbese Philip, "The Disappearing Debate: Racism and Censorship," in *Language in Her Eye: Views on Writing and Gender by Canadian Women Writing in English* (Toronto: Coach House Books, 1990), 215.

7. Ibid.

8. Ibid.

9. William Patrick Kinsella, *Dance Me Outside* (Ottawa: Oberon Press, 1977).

10. Margaret Laurence, *A Bird in the House* (Toronto: McClelland and Stewart, 1974).

11. Gordon Johnston, "An Intolerable Burden of Meaning: Native People in White Fiction," in *The Native in Literature: Canadian and Comparative Perspectives*, eds. Thomas King, Cheryl Calver, and Helen Hoy (Toronto: ECW Press, 1987), 52.

12. Ibid., 62.

13. Ibid.

14. Eli Mandel, "Imagining Natives: White Perspectives on Native Peoples," in *The Native in Literature: Canadian and Comparative Perspectives*, eds. Thomas King, Cheryl Calver, and Helen Hoy (Toronto: ECW Press, 1987), 44.

15. George Woodcock, "Prairie Winters and the Metis: Rudy Wiebe and Margaret Laurence," in *Northern Spring: The Flowering of Canadian Literature* (Canada: D.W. Friesen & Sons, 1987), 95.

16. Angelika Maeser-Lemieux, "The Metis in the Fiction of Margaret Laurence: From Outcast to Consort," in *The Native in Literature: Canadian and Comparative Perspectives*, eds. Thomas King, Cheryl Calver, and Helen Hoy (Toronto: ECW Press, 1987), 116.

17. Ibid.

18. Ibid.

19. Kinsella, *Dance Me Outside*, 6.

20. Ibid., 21.

21. Ibid., 69.

22. Ibid., 79.

23. Ibid., 73.

24. Ibid., 71.

25. Ibid., 70.

26. Ibid., 71.

27. Ibid.

28. Ibid., 74.

29. Ibid., 76.

30. Ibid., 77.

31. Ibid.

32. Ibid., 78.

33. Ibid., 72.

34. Laurence, *A Bird in the House*, 114–15.
35. Ibid., 119.
36. Ibid.
37. Ibid., 114.
38. Ibid.
39. Ibid., 3.
40. Ibid.
41. Ibid., 118.
42. Ibid.
43. Ibid., 120–21.
44. Ibid., 122.
45. Ibid., 115.
46. Ibid.
47. Ibid., 116.
48. Ibid., 117.
49. Ibid., 124.
50. Ibid.
51. Ibid., 125.
52. Ibid.
53. Maeser-Lemieux, "The Metis in the Fiction of Margaret Lawrence," 125.
54. Ibid.
55. Ibid.
56. Ibid., 125–26.
57. Ibid., 125.
58. Johnston, "An Intolerable Burden of Meaning," 52.
59. Ibid.
60. *Star Phoenix*, "Charged with Murder," January 21, 1995.

Chapter Five: Maria Campbell's *Halfbreed*: A Politicized Text for Re-membering Being

1. Maria Campbell, *Halfbreed* (Toronto: McClelland and Stewart, 1973).
2. Adrienne Rich, "When We Dead Awaken: Writing as Re-vision," in *On Lies, Secrets, and Silence: Selected Prose 1966–1978* (New York: W.W. Norton, 1979), 18.
3. Neal McLeod, *Cree Narrative Memory* (Saskatoon: Purich Publishers, 2007), 54–60.

4. Ibid., 14–15.
5. Campbell, *Halfbreed*, 2.
6. Howard Adams, *Prison of Grass: Canada from a Native Point of View* (Saskatoon: Fifth House Publishers, 1975), ix.
7. Ibid.
8. Campbell, *Halfbreed*, 11.
9. Ibid., 15.
10. Ibid., 14.
11. Ibid., 15.
12. Ibid.
13. Ibid., 72–73.
14. Ibid., 16.
15. Ibid.
16. Ibid., 17.
17. Ibid.
18. Ibid., 22.
19. Ibid., 23.
20. Ibid., 32.
21. Ibid., 30.
22. Ibid., 17.
23. Ibid., 80.
24. Ibid., 47.
25. Ibid., 46.
26. Ibid.
27. Ibid., 47.
28. Ibid., 53.
29. Ibid., 58–59.
30. Ibid.
31. Ibid.
32. Ibid., 67.
33. Ibid., 27.
34. Ibid., 114.
35. Maria Campbell, interview by Hartmut Lutz, in *Contemporary Challenges: Conversations with Contemporary Canadian Native Authors* (Saskatoon: Fifth House Publishers, 1991), 41.
36. Lenore Keeshig-Tobias, interview by Hartmut Lutz, in *Contemporary Challenges: Conversations with Contemporary Canadian Native Authors* (Saskatoon: Fifth House Publishers, 1991), 83.

37. Jeannette Armstrong, interview by Hartmut Lutz, in *Contemporary Challenges: Conversations with Contemporary Canadian Native Authors* (Saskatoon: Fifth House Publishers, 1991), 25.
38. Beth Cuthand, interview by Hartmut Lutz, in *Contemporary Challenges: Conversations with Contemporary Canadian Native Authors* (Saskatoon: Fifth House Publishers, 1991), 35.
39. Jordan Wheeler, interview by Hartmut Lutz, in *Contemporary Challenges: Conversations with Contemporary Canadian Native Authors* (Saskatoon: Fifth House Publishers, 1991), 74.
40. Emma LaRocque, preface to *Writing the Circle: Native Women of Western Canada*, eds. Jeanne Perreault and Sylvia Vance (Edmonton, AB: NeWest Publishers, 1990), xviii.

Chapter Six: Re-calling Indigenous Signifying Female Relations to Transform Being

1. Kateri Akiwenzie-Damm, "this is where we stand our ground," in *Gatherings VII*, eds. Kateri Akiwenzie-Damm and Jeannette Armstrong (Penticton, BC: Theytus Books, 1996) 1–2.
2. Ibid.
3. Christine Welsh, *Finding Dawn* (Vancouver: National Film Board of Canada, 2006), 73 min.
4. Jace Weaver, "Blue," in *Other Words: American Indian Literature, Law and Culture* (Norman: University of Oklahoma Press, 2001).
5. Ibid.
6. Ibid.
7. Akiwenzie-Damm, "this is where we stand our ground," 1–2.
8. Ibid.
9. Ibid.

Selected Bibliography

Acoose, Janice. "Deconstructing Five Generations of White Christian Patriarchal Rule" in *Residential Schools: The Stolen Years*. Saskatoon: University of Saskatchewan Press, 1993.

Adams, Howard. *Prison of Grass: Canada from a Native Point of View*. Saskatoon: Fifth House Publishers, 1975.

Akiwenzie-Damm, Kateri. "this is where we stand our ground." In *Gatherings VII*, edited by Kateri Akiwenzie-Damm and Jeannette Armstrong. Penticton, BC: Theytus, 1996.

———, ed. *Without Reservation: Indigenous Erotica*. Cape Croker Reserve, ON: Kegedonce, 2003.

Akiwenzie-Damm, Kateri, and Josie Douglas, eds. *Skins: Contemporary Indigenous Writing*. Cape Croker Reserve, ON: Kegedonce, 2000.

Albers, Patricia. "New Perspectives on Plains Indian Women." In *The Hidden Half: Studies of Plains Indian Women*. Lanham, MD: University Press of America, 1983.

Allens, Pamela Gunn. *The Sacred Hoop: Recovering the Feminine in American Indian Traditions*. Boston: Beacon Press, 1986.

———, ed. *Spider Woman's Granddaughters: Traditional Tales and Contemporary Writing by Native American Women* New York: Ballantine Books, 1989.

———. *Grandmothers of the Light: A Medicine Woman's Sourcebook*. Boston: Beacon Press, 1991.

Althusser, Louis. "Ideology and Ideological State Apparatuses." In *Contemporary Critical Theory*, edited by Dan Latimer. Toronto: Harcourt Brace Jovanovich, 1989.

Anderson, Kim. *Recognition of Being: Reconstructing Native Womanhood*. Toronto: Sumach Press, 2008.

Anderson, Margaret. "Sexism and the Social Construction of Knowledge." In *Thinking about Women: Sociological Perspectives on Sex and Gender*. New York: Macmillan, 1998. 23–45.

Andrews, Isabelle. *Crooked Lake Reserves: A Study of Indian Policy in Practice from the Qu'Appelle Treaty to 1900*. MA thesis. University of Saskatchewan, 1972.

Annharte (see also Marie Annharte Baker). *Being on the Moon*. Winlaw: Polestar, 1990.

———. "Bird Clan Mother." In Annharte, *Being on the Moon*, 40.

Armstrong, Jeannette. "The Disempowerment of First North American Native Peoples and Empowerment Through Their Writing." In *Anthropology of Canadian Native Literature in English*, edited by Daniel David Moses and Jenny Goldie, 242–45. Toronto: Oxford University Press, 1992.

———, ed. *Looking At the Words of Our People*. Penticton, BC: Theytus, 1993.

Axtell, James. *The European and the Indian: Essays in the Ethnohistory of Colonial North America*. Oxford: Oxford University Press, 1981.

Baker, Marie Annharte. *Blueberry Canoe*. Vancouver: New Star, 2001.

———. "Borrowing Enemy Language: A First Nation Woman's Use of English." In *Words in Common: Essays on Language, Culture, and Society*, edited by Gillian Thomas. Don Mills, ON: Addison-Wesley, 1999.

———. *Coyote Columbus Café*. Winnipeg, MB: Moonprint, 1994.

———. *Exercises in Lip Pointing*. Vancouver: New Star, 2003.

———. "Medicine Lines: The Doctoring of Story and Self." *Canadian Woman Studies* 14, no. 2 (1994): 114–18.

———. *Slash*. Penticton, BC: Theytus Books, 1988.

Baron, Laurie. "The CCF and the Development of Metis Colonies in Southern Saskatchewan During the Premiership of T.C. Douglas, 1944–1961." *The Canadian Journal of Native Studies* 10, no. 2 (1990): 243–70.

Benton-Banai, Edward. *The Mishomis Book: The Voice of the Ojibway*. Wisconsin: Indian Country Communications, 1988.

Berkhofer, Robert F. *The Whiteman's Indian: Images of the American Indian from Columbus to the Present*. New York: Vintage Books, 1979.

Blaeser, Kimberly. *Absentee Indians and Other Poems*. East Lansing: Michigan State University Press, 2002.

———. *Gerald Vizenor: Writing in the Oral Tradition*. Norman: University of Oklahoma Press, 1996.

———. Interview by Jennifer Andrews. "Living History: A Conversation with Kimberly Blaeser." *Studies in American Indian Literatures* 19, no. 2 (2007): 1–21.

———. "Native Literature: Seeking a Critical Center." In *Looking At the Words of Our People*. Penticton, BC: Theytus, 1993.

———, ed. "Of Landscape and Narrative." *Stories Migrating Home: A Collection of Anishinaabe Prose*. Bemidji: Loonfeather Press, 1999.

———. "Pagans Rewriting the Bible: Heterodoxy and the Representation of Spirituality in Native American Literature." *ARIEL: A Review of International English Literature* 25, no. 1 (1994): 12–31.

———. "Sacred Journey Cycles: Pilgrimage as Re-Turning and Re-Telling in American Indigenous Literatures." *Religion and Literature* 35, no. 2–3 (2003): 83–104.

———, ed. *Stories Migrating Home: A Collection of Anishinaabe Prose.* Bemidji: Loonfeather Press, 1999.

———. "Writing Voices Speaking: Native Authors and an Oral Aesthetic." In *Talking on the Page: Editing Aboriginal Texts,* edited by Laura Murray and Keren Rice, 53–68. Toronto: University of Toronto Press, 1999.

Bourgeault, Ronald. "Women in Egalitarian Society." *The New Breed Journal* (1983): 3–8.

Brown, Joseph. *The Spiritual Legacy of the American Indian.* New York: The Crossroad Publishing Company, 1992.

Buffalohead, Priscilla. "Farmers Warriors Traders: A Fresh Look At Ojibway Women." *Minnesota History* 48 (1983): 236–44.

Cameron, Anne. *Daughter of Copper Woman.* Vancouver: Press Gang Publishers, 1981.

Cameron, Deborah, ed. *The Feminist Critique of Language: A Reader.* London: Routledge, 1990.

Campbell, Maria. *Halfbreed.* Toronto: McClelland and Stewart, 1973.

Cappon, Paul, ed. *In Our Own House: Social Perspectives on Canadian Literature.* Toronto: McClelland and Stewart, 1978.

Carter, Sarah. *Lost Harvests: Prairie Indian Reserve Farmers and Government Policy.* Montreal: McGill-Queen's University Press, 1990.

Charnley, Kerrie. "Concepts of Anger, Identity and Power and the Vision in the Writings and the Voices of First Nations Women." *Gatherings: The En 'Owkin Journal of First North American Peoples* 1 (1990): 11–22.

Cook-Lynn, Elizabeth. *Why I Can't Read Wallace Stegner and Other Essays.* Madison: University of Wisconsin Press, 1996.

Cornillon, Susan Koppelman, ed. *Images of Women in Fiction: Feminist Perspectives.* Bowling Green, OH: Popular Press, 1972.

Crow Dog, Mary, and Richard Erdoes. *Lakota Woman.* New York: HarperCollins, 1990.

Culleton, Beatrice. *In Search of April Raintree.* Winnipeg, MB: Pemmican Publications, 1983.

Cuthand, Beth. *Voices in the Waterfall.* Vancouver: Lazara Press, 1989.

Dumont, Marilyn. *A Really Good Brown Girl.* London, ON: Brick Books, 1996.

Erdrich, Louise. *The Beet Queen.* Toronto: Bantam Books, 1986.

———. *Four Souls.* New York: HarperCollins, 2004.

————. *Love Medicine*. Toronto: Bantam Books, 1984.

————. *Tracks*. New York: Harper & Row, 1988.

Fanon, Frantz. *The Wretched of the Earth*. New York: Grove Press, 1963.

Fanon, Frantz. *Black Skin, White Masks*. New York: Grove Press, 1967.

————. *The Wretched of the Earth*. New York: Grove Press, 1963.

Fife, Connie, ed. *The Colour of Resistance: A Contemporary Collection of Writing by Aboriginal Women*. Toronto: Sister Vision Press, 1993.

Fitz-Gibbon, Mary, trans. *The Diaries of Edmund Montague Morris: Western Journeys 1907–1910*. Toronto: Royal Ontario Museum, 1995.

Foster, Tol. "Of One Blood: An Argument for Relations and Regionality in Native American Literary Studies." In *Reasoning Together: The Native Critics Collective*, edited by Craig Womack, Daniel Heath Justice, and Christopher Tueton, 265–302. Oklahoma: Oklahoma University Press, 2008.

Fulton, Keith Louise. "Feminism and Humanism: Margaret Laurence and the Crises of Imagination." In *Crossing the River: Essays in Honour of Margaret Laurence*, edited by Kristjana Gunnars. Winnipeg: Turnstone Press, 1988.

Gaber-Katz, Elaine, and Jenny Horseman. "Is It Her Voice If She Speaks Their Words?" *Canadian Woman Studies* 9 (1988): 117–20.

Gallerie: Women Artist's Monographs. *Give Back: First Nations Perspectives on Cultural Practice*. Vancouver: Gallerie Productions, 1992.

Gill, Sam D. *Mother Earth: An American Story*. Chicago: University of Chicago Press, 1987.

Godard, Barbara Thompson. "Talking about Ourselves: The Literary Productions of Native Women in Canada." CRIAW Paper no. ii, 1985.

Grant, Agnes, ed. *Our Bit of Truth: An Anthology of Canadian Native Literature*. Winnipeg, MB: Pemmican Publications, 1990.

Green, Rayna. "The Pocahontas Perplex: The Image of Indian Women in American Culture." In *Sweetgrass*, edited by Lenore Keeshig-Tobias. Toronto: Sweetgrass Arts Incorporated, 1984. 17–23.

Gross, Lawrence. "*Bimaadiziwin*, or the 'Good Life,' as a Unifying Concept of Anishinaabe Religion." *American Indian Culture and Research Journal* 26, no. 1 (2002). 15–32.

————. "The Comic Vision of Anishinaabe Culture and Religion." *American Indian Culture and Research Journal* 26, no. 3 (2002): 15–32.

————. "Cultural Sovereignty and Native American Hermeneutics in the Interpretation of the Sacred Stories of the Anishinaabe." *Wicazo Sa Review* (Fall 2003): 127–34.

Halfe, Louise. *Bear Bones and Feathers*. Regina, SK: Coteau, 1994.

Harjo, Joy, and Gloria Bird, eds. *Reinventing the Enemy's Language: Contemporary Native Women's Writings of North America*. New York: Norton & Company, 1977.

Highway, Tomson. Preface to *The Dispossessed*, by Geoffrey York. London: Vintage UK, 1990.

———. *Dry Lips Oughta Move to Kapuskasing*. Saskatoon: Fifth House Publishing, 1990.

hooks, bell. *Talking Back: Thinking Feminist, Thinking Black*. Toronto: Between the Lines, 1988.

———. *Yearning: Race, Gender, and Cultural Politics*. Toronto: Between the Lines, 1990.

Hryniuk, Margaret. "They Have Taken Our Land, Now Want Our Words." *Leader Post*, April 19, 1990, 6.

Hughes, Kenneth James. *Signs of Literature: Language, Ideology and the Literary Text*. Vancouver: Talonbooks, 1986.

Hulan, Renée, ed. *Native North America: Critical and Cultural Perspectives*. Toronto: ECW Press, 1999.

Independent Commission on International Humanitarian Issues. *Indigenous Peoples: A Global Quest for Justice*. London: Zed Books, 1987.

Innes, Robert. "The Importance of Family Ties to Cowessess First Nation." Diss., University of Arizona, 2007.

Johnson, Basil. *Anishinaubae Thesaurus*. East Lansing: Michigan State University Press, 2007.

———. *Crazy Dave*. Toronto: Key Porter Books, 1999.

———. "How Do We Learn Language? What Do We Learn?" In *Taking on the Page: Editing Aboriginal Oral Texts*, edited by Laura J. Murray and Keren Rice, 43–51. Toronto: University of Toronto Press, 1999.

———. *The Manitous: The Spiritual World of the Ojibway*. Toronto: Key Porter, 1995.

———. *Ojibway Ceremonies*. Toronto: McClelland & Stewart, 1982.

Johnston, Gordon. "An Intolerable Burden of Meaning: Native People in White Fiction." In *The Native in Literature: Canadian and Comparative Perspectives*, edited by Thomas King, Cheryl Calver, and Helen Hoy, 50–65. Toronto: ECW Press, 1987.

Justice, Daniel Heath. *Our Fire Survives the Storm: A Cherokee Literary History*. Minneapolis: University of Minnesota Press, 2006.

Kahgegagahbowh (see also George Copway). *The Traditional History and Characteristic Sketches of the Ojibway Nation*. Toronto: Prospero, 2001.

Kane, Margo. *"Moonlodge."* In *An Anthology of Canadian Native Literature in English*, edited by Daniel David Moses and Terry Goldie, 278–91. Toronto: Oxford University Press, 1992.

Keeshig-Tobias, Lenore. Interview in *Contemporary Challenges: Conversations with Contemporary Canadian Native Authors*, edited by Hartmut Lutz, 79–88. Saskatoon: Fifth House, 1991.

————. "Stop Stealing Native Stories." *The Globe and Mail*, January 26, 1990, 7.

King, Jonathon C.. "Wool Shirt of Louis O'soup." http://www.britishmuseum.org/explore/young_explorers/discover/museum_explorer/americas/leaders_and_rulers/wool_shirt_of_louis_osoup.aspx

King, Thomas, ed. *All My Relations: An Anthology of Contemporary Canadian Fiction*. Toronto: McClelland and Stewart, 1990.

————, ed. *Canadian Fiction Magazine* 60 (1987).

King, Thomas, Cheryl Calver, and Helen Hoy, eds. *The Native in Literature*. Toronto: ECW Press, 1987.

Kinsella, William Patrick. *Dance Me Outside*. Ottawa: Oberon Press, 1977.

Krupat, Arnold. *The Voice in the Margin: Native American Literature and the Canon*. Berkeley: University of California Press, 1989.

Lachapelle, Caroline. "Beyond Barriers: Native Women and the Women's Movement." In *Still Ain't Satisfied: Canadian Feminism Today*, edited by Maureen Fitzgerald, Connie Guberman, and Margie Wolfe, 257–64. Toronto: Women's Educational Press.

Laurence, Margaret. *A Bird in the House*. Toronto: McClelland and Stewart, 1985.

LaDuke, Winona. *Last Standing Woman*. Stillwater, HN: Voyageur Press, 1997.

LaRocque, Emma. *Defeathering the Indian*. Toronto: Book Society of Canada, 1975.

————. "Tides, Towns and Trains." In *Living the Changes*, edited by Joan Turner, 76–90. Winnipeg: University of Manitoba Press, 1990.

————. Preface to *Writing the Circle: Native Women of Western Canada*, edited by Jeanne Perreault and Sylvia Vance. Edmonton: NeWest Publishers, 1990. xv–xxix

Leacock, Eleanor. "Montagnais Women and the Jesuit Program for Colonization." In *Myths of Male Dominance: Collected Articles on Women Cross-Culturally*, 43–62. New York: Monthly Review Press, 1981.

Littlefield, Lorraine. "Women Traders in the Maritime Fur Trade." In *Native People, Native Lands: Canadian Indians, Inuit and Metis*, edited by Bruce Aldon Cox, 173–83. Ottawa: Carleton Univeristy Press, 1987.

Lutz, Hartmut. "The Circle as Philosophical and Structural Concept in Native American Fiction Today." In *Native American Literature*, 85–99. Pisa, Italy: Servizio Editoriale Universitario, 1989.

————, ed. *Contemporary Challenges: Conversations with Contemporary Canadian Native Writers*. Saskatoon: Fifth House Publishers, 1991.

————. "Indians' and Native Americans in the Movies: A History of Stereotypes, Distortions, and Displacements." *Visual Anthropology* 3 (1990): 31–46.

McGill, Jean. *Edmund Morris: Frontier Artist*. Toronto: Dundurn Press, 1984.

McLeod, Neal. "Coming Home Through Stories." In *(Ad)dressing Our Words: Aboriginal Perspectives on Aboriginal Literatures*, edited by Armand Garnet Rufflo. Penticton: Theytus Books, 2001. 17–35.

————. *Cree Narrative Memory: From Treaties to Contemporary Times*. Saskatoon: Purich Publishers, 2007.

McKegney, Sam. *Magic Weapons: Aboriginal Writers Remaking Community after Residential School*. Winnipeg: University of Manitoba Press, 2007.

McQuire, Patricia. *Restorative Dispute Resolution in Anishinaabe Communities— Restoring Conceptions of Relationships Based on Dodem*. National Centre for First Nations Governance. http://fngovernance.org/ncfng_research/patricia_mcguire.pdf.

Maeser-Lemieux, Angelika. "The Metis in the Fiction of Margaret Laurence: From Outcast to Consort." In *The Native in Literature: Canadian and Comparative Perspectives*, edited by Thomas King, Cheryl Calver, and Helen Hoy, 115–29. Toronto: ECW Press, 1987.

Mandel, Eli. "Imagining Natives: White Perspectives on Native Peoples." *In The Native in Literature: Canadian and Comparative Perspectives*, edited by Thomas King, Cheryl Calver, and Helen Hoy, 34–47. Toronto: ECW Press, 1987.

Maracle, Lee. *Bobbi Lee: Indian Rebel*. Toronto: Women's Press, 1990.

————. *I Am Woman*. Vancouver: Write-on Press Publishers, 1988.

————. *Sojourner's Truth & Other Stories*. Vancouver: Press Gang Publishers, 1990.

Medicine, Beatrice. "'Warrior Women'—Sex Role Alternatives for Plains Indian Women." In *The Hidden Half: Studies of Plains Indian Women*. Lanham, MD: University Press of America, 1983.

Meyer, Melissa. *The White Earth Tragedy: Ethnicity and Dispossession at a Minnesota Anishinaabe Reservation*. Lincoln: University of Nebraska Press, 1994.

Mihesuah, Devon, and Angela Cavender Wilson. "Activism and Apathy: The Prices We Pay." *American Indian Quarterly* 27, no. 1–2 (2003). 325–32.

————. "Finding Empowerment through Writing and Reading, or Why am I Doing This?: An Unpopular Writer's Comment about the State of American Indian Criticism." *American Indian Quarterly* 28, no. 1–2 (2008). 97–102.

————, eds. *Indigenizing the Academy: Transforming Scholarship and Empowering Communities*. Lincoln: Nebraska University Press, 2004.

————. *So You Want to Write About American Indians?: A Guide for Writers, Students, and Scholars*. Lincoln: University of Nebraska Press, 2005.

Mitchell, W.O. *Jake and the Kid*. Toronto: McClelland and Stewart, 1985.

Monkman, Leslie. *A Native Heritage: Images of the Indian in English-Canadian Literature*. Toronto: University of Toronto Press, 1981.

————. "The Tonnerre Family: Mirrors of Suffering." *Journal of Canadian Fiction* (1980): 27.

Monture-Angus, Patricia. "Native America and the Literary Tradition." In *Native North America: Critical and Cultural Perspectives*, edited by Renée Hulan. Toronto: ECW Press, 1999. 20–46.

Morris, Alexander. *The Treaties of Canada with the Indians of Manitoba and the North-West Territories including the Negotiations on which they were based*. Calgary: Fifth House, 1991.

Morris, Edmund Montague (see also Fitz-Gibbon, Mary). *Diaries*.

"Mother Earth." *CBC Ideas*. Toronto. June 5, 2003. qspace.library.queensu.ca.

Native Women's Association of Canada. "Sisters in Spirit." Report of Missing and Murdered Aboriginal Women in Canada, 2010.

New, William H. *A History of Canadian Literature*. London: Macmillan Education, 1989.

————. *Native Writers and Canadian Writing: Canadian Literature Special Issue*. Vancouver: University of British Columbia Press, 1990.

Newman, Peter. *Company of Adventurers*. Toronto: Penguin, 1985.

Noori, Margaret. *Native American Literature in Tribal Context: Anishinaabe Aadisokaanag Noongom*. Diss., University of Minnesota, 2001.

Nourbese Philip, Marlene. "The Disappearing Debate: Racism and Censorship." In *Language in Her Eye: Views on Writing and Gender by Canadian Women Writing in English*, 215. Toronto: Coach House Books, 1990.

Obomsawin, Alanis. *Kanehsatake 270 Years Of Resistance*. NFB, 1993.

Osennontion and Skonaganleh:ra. "Our World: According to Osennontion and Skonaganleh:ra." *Canadian Woman Studies/les cahiers de la femme* (Summer/Fall 1989), 7–19.

Ostenso, Martha. *Wild Geese*. Toronto: McClelland and Stewart, 1961.

Petrone, Penny. *Native Literature in Canada: From the Oral Tradition to the Present*. Toronto: Oxford University Press, 1990.

Powers, Marla. "Sex Roles and Social Structures." In *Myth, Ritual, and Reality*, 203–14. Chicago: Chicago University Press, 1983.

RCMP Report on Missing and Murdered Aboriginal Women: A National Operational Overview. Royal Canadian Mounted Police, 2014. http://www.rcmp-grc.gc.ca/pubs/mmaw-faapd-eng.pdf

Rich, Adrienne. "When We Dead Awaken: Writing as Re-vision." In *On Secrets, Lies and Silence: Selected Prose 1966–1978*. New York: W.W. Norton, 1979.

Rockwell, Joan. "A Theory of Literature in Society: The Hermeneutic Approach." *Sociological Review Monograph* 25 (August 1977): 32–42.

Ross, Rupert. *Dancing with a Ghost: Exploring Indian Reality*. Markham, ON: Reed Books Canada, 1992.

Scott, Duncan Campbell. "Lines in Memory of Edmund Morris." In *Lundy's Lane and Other Poems*. Toronto: McClelland and Stewart, 1916. 179–94.

Smith, Linda Tuhiwai. *Decolonizing Methodologies*. London: Zed, 1999.

Smits, David D. "The 'Squaw Drudge': A Prime Index of Savagism." *Ethnohistory* 29 (1982): 281–301.

Stedman, Raymond William. *Shadows of the Indian: Stereotypes in American Culture*. Norman: University Press of Oklahoma, 1989.

Stegner, Wallace. *Wolf Willow*. Lincoln: University Press of Nebraska, 1980.

Stevenson, Winona. "'Ethnic' Assimilates 'Indigenous': A Study in Intellectual Neocolonialism." *Wicazo Review: A Journal of Native American Studies* (Spring 1998): 33–51.

Sutherland, Ronald. *Second Image: Comparative Studies in Quebec/Canadian Literature*. Toronto: New Press, 1971.

Suzack, Cheryl. "Land Claims, Identity Claims: Mapping Indigenous Feminism in Literary Criticism and in Winnona LaDuke's *Last Standing Woman*." *Reasoning Together: The Native Critics Collective*, edited by Craig Womack, Daniel Heath Justice, and Christopher Tueton. Oklahoma: Oklahoma University Press, 2008. 169–92.

Swann, Brian, and Arnold Krupat, eds. *Recovering the Word: Essays on Native American Literature*. Berkeley: University of California Press, 1983.

Tarasoff, J. Koozma. *Persistent Ceremonialism: The Plains Cree and Saulteaux*. Ottawa: National Museums of Canada, 1980.

Thiong'o, Ngugi Wa. *Writers in Politics*. London: Heinemann Educational Books, 1981.

Thomas, Clara. "'Planted firmly in some soil': Margaret Laurence and the Canadian Tradition in Fiction." In *Critical Approaches to the Fiction of Margaret Laurence*, edited by Colin Nicholson, 1–14. Vancouver: University of British Columbia Press, 1990.

Thwaites, R. G. *Jesuit Relations and Allied Documents.* 73 vols. New York: Pageant Books, 1959.

United Nations General Assembly. *United Nations Declaration on the Rights of Indigenous Peoples,* October 2, 2007, A/RES/61/295.

Ussher, Jane. *The Psychology of the Female Body.* London: Routledge, 1989.

Vangen, Kate. "Making Faces: Defiance and Humour in Campbell's *Halfbreed* and Welch's *Winter in the Blood.*" In *The Native in Literature: Canadian and Comparative Perspectives,* edited by Thomas King, Cheryl Calver, and Helen Hoy, 188–203. Toronto: ECW Press, 1987.

Van Kirk, Sylvia. *Many Tender Ties: Women in Fur Trade Society, 1670–1870.* Winnipeg, MB: Watson and Dwyer, 1980.

———. "'Women in Between': Indian Women in Fur Trade Society in Western Canada." In *Out of the Background: Readings in Canadian Native History.* Toronto: Copp Clark Pitman, 1988. 150–63.

Wagamese, Richard. *Indian Horse.* Vancouver: Douglas and McIntyre, 2012.

Waubageshig, ed. *The Only Good Indian.* Toronto: New Press, 1970.

Warrior, Robert. *The People and the Word: Reading Native Nonfiction.* Minneapolis: University of Minnesota Press, 2005.

———. *Tribal Secrets: Recovering American Indian Intellectual Traditions.* Minneapolis: University of Minnesota Press, 1995.

Weaver, Jace, Craig Womack, and Robert Warrior. *American Indian Literary Separatism.* Albuquerque: New Mexico University Press, 2006.

———. *Other Words: American Indian Literature, Law and Culture.* Norman: University of Oklahoma Press, 2001.

———. *That the People Might Live: Native American Literature and Native American Community.* New York: Oxford University Press, 1997.

Weedon, Chris. *Feminist Practice & Poststructuralist Theory.* London: Basil Blackwell, 1988.

Wiebe, Rudy. "Proud Cree Nation Deserves Much More Than Funny Stories." *The Globe and Mail,* February 17, 1990, 3.

Wilkinson, Gerald. "Colonialism in the Media." *The Indian Historian* 7 (1974): 29–32.

Wilson, Angela Cavender. "Reclaiming Our Humanity: Decolonization and the Recovery of Indigenous Knowledge." In *Indigenizing the Academy: Transforming Scholarship and Empowering Communities,* edited by Devon Abbott Mihesuah and Angela Cavender Wilson. Lincoln: University of Nebraska Press, 2004. 69–87.

Wilson, Shawn. *Research Is Ceremony: Indigenous Research Methods.* Halifax, NS: Fernwood, 2008.

Witalec, Janet, ed. *Native North American Literature*. Toronto: Gale, 1994.

Wolfe, Alexander, teller. *Earth Elder Stories: The Pinayzitt Path*. Saskatoon: Fifth House, 1988.

Wolff, Janet. "Art as Ideology." In *The Social Production of Art*. London: Macmillan Education, 1981.

Woodcock, George. "Prairie Writers and the Metis: Rudy Wiebe and Margaret Laurence." In *Northern Spring: The Flowering of Canadian Literature*, 94–109. Winnipeg, MB: D.W. Freisen & Sons, 1987.

Womack, Craig. "Afterwards: Theorizing American Indian Experience." In *Reasoning Together: The Native Critics Collective*, edited by Craig Womack, Daniel Heath Justice, and Christopher Tueton. Norman: Oklahoma University Press, 2008. 353–410.

———. "Introduction: A Single Decade: Book-Length Native Literary Criticism between 1986 and 1997." *Reasoning Together: The Native Critics Collective*, edited by Craig Womack, Daniel Heath Justice, and Christopher Tueton. Norman: Oklahoma University Press, 2008. 3–104.

———. *Reasoning Together: The Native Critics Collection*, edited by Craig Womack, Daniel Heath Justice, and Chris Tueton, 3–104. Norman: Oklahoma University Press, 2008.

———. *Red on Red: Native American Literary Separatism*. Minneapolis: University of Minneapolis Press, 1999.

Woodcock, George. "Prairie Writers and the Metis: Rudy Wiebe and Margaret Laurence." In *Northern Spring: The Flowering of Canadian Literature*, 94–109. Winnipeg, MB: D.W. Freisen & Sons, 1987.

York, Geoffrey. *The Dispossessed*. London: Vintage UK, 1990.

Copyright Acknowledgements